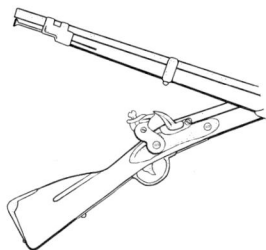

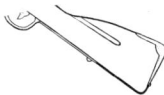

An UPDATE on

Landguard Fort

Felixstowe

in

Suffolk

by

Doreen Rayner

Best Wishes,
Doreen Rayner

Published in Great Britain by
Doreen Rayner,
8 Manor Terrace,
Felixstowe,
Suffolk,
IP11 8EN

© 1995 Doreen Rayner

ISBN 0-9527153-0-9

British Library Cataloguing-in-Publication Data.
A catalogue record of this book is available from the British Library.

Designed and set by
ARIOMA,
Gloucester House, High Street,
BORTH, Dyfed, SY24 5HZ
Tel/Fax (01970) 871296

Printed by
Cambrian Printers,
Llanbadarn Road,
ABERYSTWYTH,
Dyfed, SY23 3TN

Cover design by ARIOMA. Photograph *Bunny Rayner*
Front: Fort Interior. Back: The Author in the outer courtyard.

View of Fort Interior

Unchanged since 1875 except for the drawbridge which was replaced by a causeway just prior to World War II

The Granite surrounding the entrance to inner courtyard is said to have arrived by barge from Cornwall.

Photograph: Bunny Rayner

FOREWORD

Doreen Rayner's appeal, in November 1992, for people with personal or family connections with Landguard Fort to contact her, stirred me to action.

As a result of indefatigable work with The Felixstowe History and Museum Society, hers is a name which will always be associated with any history of the fort, and the news that she is to write a book about it should rally people to help.

'Time,' wrote Isaac Watts, 'like an ever rolling stream, bears all its sons away,' - and with us our accumulated knowledge and recollections, if we do not do something about it in good time.

A new tapestry is about to be woven and perhaps my experiences might add marginal strength to its warp and weft?

Having established that Mrs Rayner's remit covers all the Landguard peninsular and not just the fort and that she intends to make her book more human interest than military history, I was encouraged to sort out my jumbled recollections of life at Landguard Common during the decade preceding the 1939-1945 war, when I was nine to nineteen.

An explanation as to why a nine-year-old Ipswich boy felt drawn to this area, and became fascinated with it, is to be found in a chapter headed "The Lure of Landguard, 1929-1939".

John C. Butters, Dipl. Arch., RIBA (Ret.)

ACKNOWLEDGEMENTS

I am indebted to friends and interested colleagues for their contributions to UPDATE, particularly John Butters, who has offered a great deal of information on the period between 1929 and 1939.

Sincere thanks go to D. Bewers, B. Burgoyne, D. Burt, F. Glover, G. Cordy, my neighbour, Ron Gleed, J. Jackson, Dr. I. Reid, J.Roper, the Rutterford brothers, W. E. Watts, David.Wood, The Port of Felixstowe and others not mentioned on this page, but whose help, even so, has been greatly appreciated.

Doreen Rayner
Author
1995

CONTENTS

Foreword by John Butters	IV
Acknowledgements	V
List of Illustrations	VIII
Introduction	X
Landguard Discovered 1975	1
The Monument ... Some Historical Facts	5
Surgeons and Medical Officers	10
The Redoubt	11
Thomas Hyde Page	11
Batteries	14
The Area - 1903	15
Landguard Lodge and Lt. F. H. Yorke	16
Fire Command Post - 1904	23
First World War	28
The Lure of Landguard 1920s/1930s	43
The Warden - Harry Vines	47
Guns and Gun Crews - 1940	48
Balloon Busters	54
Extracts from 1939/45 Diary by Ernest Joseph Hill	60
HMS Beehive	67
German Surrender	72
District Gunners	73
Rough Riders	74
Gas Buses	74
Darell Day	74
The Ravelin Block	75

Engine Room and Searchlights   80
Operations Room - 1951   81
Seaward Defence Headquarters   82
419 Coast Regiment   86
Landguard Fort Trust   87
Ancient Fortifications   89
The Old Fort   90
The New Fort   91

ILLUSTRATIONS

Fort Interior.	III
King's Bastion. Waist high weeds and grasses.	3
Barrack Block - 1730's.	4
Landguard Lodge. Former Officers Mess.	17
Casemated Battery. 1870's.	21
Inner Courtyard.	22
Sketch of Fire Command Post.	24
Landguard Football Team 1904.	25
Garrison Members. 1910.	26
Suffolk Cyclists & Cook House, Landguard Common 1911.	26
Mortar Gun Crew. 1st WW. Landguard Common.	32
War-time pass.	27
Bomb-damaged houses, Garrison Lane, 1917.	27
Air-Raid Damage. 1917. Blacksmith Shop and Ordnance Hotel.	29
Crashed Zeppelin L 48, 1917.	30
"C" Company. 4th Vol. Bat. Suffolk Regiment, December 1918	33
Royal Naval Air Station Football Team, 1915/16.	35
Map of the Rifle Ranges. 1930's.	36
Musketry Office. 1930's.	39
Camouflaged Searchlight Post. 1930's.	40
Right Battery. 1930's.	41

Tide Indicator.	42
Range Warden.	46
Floating Targets.	46
Bleak Outpost. 1940.	49
Interior of Victorian Gun Battery.	50
On Parade. Inner Courtyard. 1940.	56
Barbers Shop. 1940.	57
Bomb Damage, Felixstowe Ferry.	63
Wrens. Suffolk Convalescent Home Billets.	69
Boom Defence. 1943.	
Crashed Aircraft. Coastguard Cottages.	71
Surrender of German E Boats. 1945.	72
Ravelin Block, 1980.	76
Vandalised Interior, Ravelin Block.	78
"P" and "S" Batteries 419 Coast Regiment	85

INTRODUCTION

Nearing the end of September, 1896, Major John Henry Leslie, expecting to move to Landguard Fort, Felixstowe, Suffolk, in October of that same year, paid a short visit to the town and Landguard Point.

On the return journey to Shoeburyness he stopped for the night at Ipswich to dine with a friend at his house there. In the course of after-dinner conversation, his host, Hon. Colonel J. H. Josselyn of the 1st. Volunteer Battalion, the Suffolk Regiment, suggested Leslie should write a short history about the place. 'Thus,' wrote the Major, a few months later, 'was the book The History of Landguard Fort in Suffolk conceived.'

It was published by Eyre and Spottiswoode in 1898, selling at a price of twelve shillings per copy. Today the same book will cost somewhere in the region of one hundred pounds!

The last paragraph in Major Leslie's book reads:

'As regards the present armament of Landguard Fort I must perforce maintain complete silence. I may, however, venture to express an opinion that its present construction and armament are both of them such that a modern enemy would still find this bulwark of the most important harbour between the Thames and the Humber as hard a nut to crack as it was discovered to be by our Dutch foeman in the bygone days when the merry monarch was king, and when his able officer, Darell, so successfully repelled their bold attack upon it in July of 1667.'

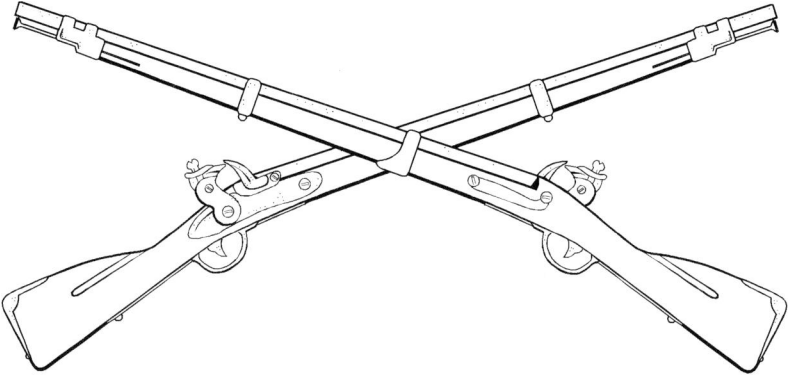

XIII

LANDGUARD DISCOVERED 1975

The name Landguard is a corruption of Lunger, which in turn stems from the more ancient Langestuna, meaning Long Stone, or a narrow finger of land jutting out and into the sea upon which local fishermen once cleaned their nets and laid them out to dry.

Men still fish at Landguard, although it may no longer be described as a bleak, isolated spot, since the area supports the largest 18th century fortification on the east coast, together with a popular museum, Nature Reserve and Bird Observatory. One of two small car parks has recently been extended, courtesy of the Port of Felixstowe, to accommodate an additional sixty vehicles. It overlooks the rivers Stour and Orwell, and has been named the John Bradfield Viewing Area.

The first known fortifications at Landguard (blockhouses) were built at the express command of Henry VIII. They were constructed on a then vulnerable stretch of coastline to meet the threat of invasion by two powerful Catholic countries, namely Rome and France.

Following the Armada scare in 1588, the blockhouses fell into a state of disrepair. Lunger Poynte, therefore, remained undefended until 1626, when a new fort was built. This larger, stronger construction was destined to play a significant part in the wars against the Dutch who landed on the Felixstowe beaches and attacked the fort in 1667.

A detailed account of this most important battle has been written by Frank Hussey, whose book is entitled *Suffolk Invasion*.

The author discovered Landguard Fort one long ago summer afternoon while strolling across a considerably larger stretch of common land than exists today.

The panoramic view from atop a grass covered mound, later discovered to be the 19th century Left Battery, was breathtaking. It took in the towns of Shotley, Harwich, Dovercourt and Walton-on-the-Naze on the opposite side of the rivers, and a wide expanse of ocean known as the North Sea.

In 1975 there were many acres of Ministry of Defence land, outbuildings and former married quarters once housing service families. There was also a growing Felixstowe dock.

In a hollow to the left was a large building sporting weather-beaten, grey, asphalted roof tops. The author descended from her vantage point to obtain a closer look.

So began an interest in a coastal fortification which has, over a long period of time, delivered up to the writer an amazing amount of historical data. Landguard's ancient, historical past has, of course, been well documented. Information contained in this small book, however, has for the most part come by way of personal contact with those who lived or served here between the 1914/18 and 1939/45 wars.

The remainder of the afternoon was spent wandering

round the fortification by way of a wide ditch designed centuries ago to deter an enemy force. A sort of no-man's-land.

It was once laid to lawn and planted with trees, including the Tamarisk, which is said to have been introduced to Landguard by Philip Thicknesse, Lieutenant Governor from 1753-1766.

In 1975, however, waist-high weeds and grasses covered brick rubble, rubbish and even a pair of huge wrought iron gates.

1975 Waist high weeds and grasses.
King's Bastion, foreground: Holland Bastion, background.

Photograph Bunny Rayner

These were retrieved by an enthusiastic group of History Society members who, having discovered their original home, returned them to the main corridor of the nearby, nineteen-room, 19th century Ravelin Block, which had by 1980 become their headquarters, courtesy of the Department of the Environment.

The ditch has since been cleared and laid with shingle. It is regularly maintained by English Heritage, who are custodians of the building.

Note: See chapter headed RAVELIN BLOCK.

Barrack Block of the 1740's
Turret clock, top left of photograph.

THE MONUMENT ....
SOME HISTORICAL FACTS

The existing fortification is referred to as "the new fort". It began life as a sea battery, with between sixteen and twenty guns, in about 1716.

In 1731, a barrack block with adjoining hospital was extended and raised to three storeys, and, by 1744, eighteen feet high walls with four angled bastions and a south tower had been built to enclose all of the above-mentioned, plus a spacious three storey residence for the Lieutenant Governor and his family.

A chapel constructed above the main gateway was said to be capable of seating three hundred people. Philip Thicknesse described the chapel as being:

'A great room, at one end a desk, a pulpit and pews. At the other end a great window, under that window a table to administer the sacrament from, elevated above the floor and railed off.'

It was from the Landguard Fort chapel that a burial service was conducted for Philip's second wife, Elizabeth, who died in March of 1762 at her seafront cottage home (Cobbolds Point), following the birth of a son. Elizabeth was interred in the fort burial ground, which has since been swallowed up by encroaching seas. Philip is said to have married his third wife, Ann Ford, at Landguard Fort, in September of that same year.

Others laid to rest at Landguard included John Ancor,

Master Gunner, who died 1762, aged 86; Captain Thomas Tucker, Pembrokeshire Militia, died 1781, aged 22 years; Ensign John Roberts, died 1794, aged 65 years; Andrew McLaughlan, Store-Keeper, died 1795, aged 43 years, and Susan, his wife, died 1789, aged 33 years. John Jones, twenty-nine years resident in the garrison, died June 12th, 1806, aged 54 years .... the list goes on.

Governors and Lt. Governors, wives, children, servants, garrison members and their families, and noteworthies such as Thomas Gainsborough all attended Sunday services in the Landguard chapel.

On the ground floor, 18th century casemates, arched doorways facing a large circular courtyard, were built into the red brick walls, and remain in evidence today.

Over the years, most have been converted for various other uses, such as clean and dirty linen stores, quartermasters' stores, ration stores, wireless and telecommunications rooms, machine shops, bath houses, First Aid waiting rooms, decontamination chambers, and even a place in which to house the manual fire engine.

The fort turret clock, made by Thomas Moore of Ipswich (1720-1789), was situated above the 18th century barrack block, until its removal to a newly built clock chamber following the "great re-modelling of 1875." Its intricate mechanism was supported there by a stout wooden bench, which enabled the dial, or face, to look down upon the outer courtyard. The clock bell is inscribed ANDREAS SCHACHT 1733.

During the 1970s, this valuable timepiece was removed to Bury St. Edmunds for safe keeping. It is now in working order and on display at the Manor House museum there.

An ancient document reads: 'A list of works and repairs dated 10th April 1747. An abstract of the foregoing works and repairs humbly proposed to be carried out at Landguard Fort.

'To build a turret for a clock over the centre of the new barracks
£30.0s.0d.

'For a good eight day clock as proposed by Mr. Thos. Moore of Ipswich   £67.0s.0d.

'Total   £97.0s.0d

and

'Repairs wanted to the Govrs. lodging and old barracks
£60.3s.2d'

The "great remodelling" mentioned earlier took place between 1871 and 1875, with all interior buildings being demolished. The 18th century parade ground became divided into an inner and outer courtyard, by way of a large circular Keep.

The south tower and much of the curtain wall between Harwich and King's bastions was removed to make way for a huge casemated battery for seven powerful, rifled, muzzle-loading cannon, which remained in position until about 1906.

Beneath the battery, completely hidden from view, are 19th century magazine chambers sandwiched between magazine and lamp passages.

Today, the main entrance to Landguard is reached by a stone causeway, which replaced a wooden drawbridge in the 1930s, just prior to the second world war.

To the left of the causeway is Holland bastion, to the right Chapel bastion. The former was named for Henry Rich, Earl of Holland, who was Governor of the old 17th century fort. He was executed in 1649, for he could not make up his mind whether to support Cromwell or the King. Thomas Ireton, whose brother Henry had married Bridget Cromwell, succeeded the unfortunate Earl. He died at Landguard Fort in 1652.

Chapel bastion was named for the huge 18th century chapel once situated above the main gateway.

A Caponier, or narrow covered-in tunnel, stretching across the ditch, a solid brick, hemispherical structure attached to the end of it (built to deflect pointed shells fired from huge iron ships introduced by the French) was erected between Harwich and King's bastions.

The former looks across river towards the town of that name, while the latter was named for James or, perhaps, Charles I. Historians remain uncertain!

One October 1993, Sunday morning, a small History and Museum Society working party commenced the task of clearing rubbish from former coal stores, just inside the main entrance. Having read the transcript of a Court Martial which had taken place in 1748, the writer became convinced that the coal store to the left of the main entrance was the original 18th century "Black Hole" wherein soldiers awaiting the lash, or some other obscene form of punishment, were confined. In 1754, a sergeant re-captured after going absent without leave was incarcerated here to await execution.

A few years earlier, in August of 1748, Richard Hunt, boatman, had been imprisoned for taking the garrison rowing boat, used to ferry personnel to and from Harwich, without first asking permission of the then governor. This story is not mine to tell. Sufficient to say that strong protest was made by certain officers, who argued that since they paid the prisoner's wages, Governor Hayes had no right to inflict punishment upon him at all. Two of the officers were imprisoned for physically assaulting their superior officer, who refused to release the unfortunate prisoner.

Anthony Goode was imprisoned in the "black hole" in 1753. Goode had 'gone over the head' of the new Lieutenant Governor, Thicknesse, to bitterly complain to the Master General of the Ordnance about the damage done by 'horses grasing on the covered way' - a fact ignored by Thicknesse, who happened to be extremely fond of animals, particularly dogs and horses!

In addition, he, Thicknesse, strongly objected to his 'wings being thus clipped', and had Goode and an accomplice placed 'in the very apartment Mr. Goode has himself built, being a Master Mason, for the interment of poor invalids,' - the latter being semi-retired servicemen who were either too old, or too badly wounded, to remain part of a fighting force.

Others were constrained in this dark, airless chamber following hours of "riding the horse", a degrading form of punishment, whereby the defaulter was made to sit upon a tall wooden block in the centre of the parade ground, hands tied behind his back and heavy weights attached to his feet. When extreme pain resulted in loss of consciousness, he would be pulled from the block and returned to the cell.

During the great re-modelling of 1875, the black hole was converted into a coal store. One of the 18th century barrack rooms, arched windows overlooking the outer courtyard, became the new detention cell. The adjoining guardroom remained in use until the 1950s.

SURGEONS AND MEDICAL OFFICERS

Whilst there is no doubt that Landguard Fort received medical care from within the Army Medical Services whenever there was a Garrison of any number based on the Fort, at other times the local Surgeons were responsible. They held varying titles over the years.

1827 - 1849   Henry Wllkin.
In May 1827 he removed 15 pieces of bone from a soldier's face after a gunshot wound.

Two of Dr. Henry Wilkin's sons served as Army Surgeons in the Crimean War. John Henry Wilkin was "called out in front of his Regiment on parade, and thanked by the Commander in Chief for services in the field." He was awarded a Mention in Despatches during the Indian mutiny, 'for making a brave attempt to rescue Cornet Banks who was surrounded by the enemy and was wounded.'

Wilkin, himself, was severely wounded.

1845 - 1875   John Elliot Snow.
Acting Surgeon to Royal Artillery and Royal Engineers.

1860   John Rand. Honorary Assistant Surgeon to Artillery.

1876 - 1883   Henry Jukes Hibberd.
Civilian Surgeon. Coastal Brigade, Royal Artillery.

1883 - 1923   Charles Graham Havell.
               Civilian Surgeon to Landguard Fort.

1923 - 1939   Harpur Vernon Edwards.
               Medical Officer.

1945 - 1956   Robert Howard Reid.
               Civilian medical Officer, attached to
               Landguard Fort.

LANDGUARD REDOUBT.

By 1782, an engineer named Thomas Hyde Page had constructed various outworks and a Redoubt, this latter being without guns, since it was to be used as an additional barrack block, if it became necessary to increase defence of the fort.

It was named after Lord Townsend's seat at Rainham, in Norfolk, and was situated close to the fort burial ground, which was approximately one quarter of a mile from the main (fort) building.

The burial ground rested upon the site of an ancient Tudor blockhouse, built about 1547.

THOMAS HYDE PAGE.

In 1985, the writer received a letter from Christies Auctioneers, of London, who explained that a client was researching the connection between Thomas Hyde Page (1746-1821) and Landguard Fort. Was there information available?

The following notes, discovered in volume X1 of *FORT,* *(International Journal of Fortifications and Military Architecture)*, were duly forwarded.

'In 1778 Lord Amhurst considered Harwich to be a very proper station for a considerable part of the army in time of war with the Dutch. The Harwich town water supply was at that time insufficient, so a retrenched camp was laid out at Landguard by Captain Hyde Page with two Redoubts facing the channel.'

Thomas Hyde Page joined the Corps of Engineers in July of 1769, when he was twenty-three years old, and in 1774 was promoted to the rank of Sub-Engineer and Lieutenant, with a wage of four shillings and eight pence per day. He later became aide-de-camp to General Pigott, who served under General Howe at Bunker's Hill during the American Revolution.

Wounds received in 1775 resulted in the amputation of one foot - and a regular weekly pension of ten shillings, which was paid to him for the rest of his life. He was made a Baronet in 1783, the year in which he married his second wife, Mary Woodward. They later had three sons and two daughters. Sir Thomas Hyde Page remained involved with engineering works until his death in 1821, aged seventy-five.

This particular contact resulted in a meeting with Major Martin Gibbs (aforementioned client) and his wife, of Sheldon Manor in Wiltshire, who travelled to Felixstowe to tour Landguard Point and fort interior.

Before returning home, the Major, a great, great, great grandson of Thomas Hyde Page, presented the Felixstowe Museum with a copy portrait of his illustrious ancestor, the original of which was painted by the 18th century artist James

Northcote, who (it is thought) offered the following description of the uniform he was wearing at the time of sitting.

'His black hat has a gold button and loop, his gloves are buff. His hair is dark grey. The epaulette is gold embroidery mixed with black. The top of the boot on the right leg is brown. The sword lying on the ground has a black scabbard and steel or silver mounts. The map in his hand is clearly marked Landguard Fort.'

The copy portrait, having been enlarged and framed, adorns one of the white-painted walls in the Landguard Room at the museum.

By 1810, a Martello Tower had been built on Landguard Common and given the initial "O". N, P, Q, R, S, T and U were also built along the Felixstowe coastline, although only P, Q, T and U remain.

Martello "O" was demolished around 1822, following partial destruction by encroaching seas. Much of its material was used by John Cobbold in the building of the Hamilton Hotel in 1839. "The Hamilton" later became known as the Bath Hotel, which was destroyed by fire by militant Suffragettes in 1914.

From the Roman period in its history, Felixstowe appears to have been a military zone. Shore Forts, Norman castle, Tudor Blockhouses, Landguard fort, Redoubts, Martello Towers, Cliff-top Brackenbury fort, and offshore sea, or Churchill, forts.

BATTERIES

LEFT BATTERY
Work commenced 1888. Completed 1891.
Costs: £7,252.
One 10-inch Breech-Loading Gun. Drawing in Felixstowe Museum. Two 6-inch guns mounted 1939/45 war.
Battery filled in.

RIGHT BATTERY
Work commenced 1898. Completed 1901.
Costs: £13,950.
One 10-inch Breech-Loading Gun. Drawing in Felixstowe Museum. Two 6-inch guns mounted 1939/45 war. Became Landguard Bird Observatory 1981.

DARELL BATTERY
Originally named Beauclerk's Battery for Lord George Beauclerk, who was appointed Governor of Landguard Fort on December 25th, 1753. He held the office until his death, on May 11th, 1768.

MINEFIELD BATTERY.
Built on same site in 1902. Thought to be named for MINE CONTROL. At the time, mines were assembled and filled within the RAVELIN BLOCK, before being wheeled on trolleys down to the jetty, to be placed at intervals across the mouth of the harbour, to prevent intrusion by enemy submarines.

Re-named **DARELL BATTERY,** in the 1930s, to commemorate the defeat of the Dutch who attacked Landguard Fort in 1667. Captain Nathaniel Darell was in charge of the garrison at that time. A descriptive plaque is affixed to the battery. Two concrete turrets on either side of the battery date from the second world war. Twin 6-inch guns mounted.

MANOR HOUSE BATTERY
One thousand yards north of Right Battery, close to Landguard Lodge. Installed in the summer of 1940, it was able to cover the beach as far north as Cobbolds Point. The two 6-inch guns were dismantled at the end of the second world war.

THE AREA, 1903

The old Station Pier at Landguard Point faced Harwich. It was built in the late 1870s, at about the same time as the Pier Hotel. During the 1939/45 war, the hotel was renamed "The Little Ships" in honour of the men who manned Motor Torpedo Boats, which operated from the dock basin under the base name of HMS BEEHIVE. The hotel was demolished in 1991.

There was an additional pier, known as "the iron pier", complete with tramway leading to its head, where a beacon and crane were situated.

Twin-funnelled paddle-steamers, each carrying approximately two hundred passengers, anchored at the end of Station Pier, to allow holidaymakers and day-trippers to disembark; some to make their way to an hotel, or one of the many boarding houses springing into being all over town, others to spend a few hours window-shopping in the main thoroughfare, which had been named for the Duke of Hamilton.

Landguard barracks, canteen, water tower, water tanks, rifle ranges, oil stores and various other outbuildings were situated further along the beach and on all that part of

Landguard Common between Carr Road and the sea, with the exception of Manor Terrace and Manor Road.

Garrison members approached the fort by way of the old Landguard Road, which ran from a row of terraced houses (West End View) and across the Common to a point close to the fort entrance. One hundred yards or so past the residential properties were more latrines, water tanks and officers' and men's ablution rooms, while to the left of these were sentry and lookout posts, the butts, a Musketry office, later converted for use as a target shed, gun batteries, and a series of railway lines linking the whole.

A short distance from the iron pier and in line with Landguard's Harwich bastion was a wooden jetty associated with "Mine Control". Another railway track was laid from the Harwich Conservancy jetty to the Point; it passed the mid-nineteenth century Landguard lighthouse, which was destroyed by fire in 1925.

LANDGUARD LODGE and Lt. F. H. YORKE.

The property known as Landguard Lodge was built in Manor Terrace in the late 1870s. It is not shown on the map dated 1903, although an Officers' mess and quarters are indicated.

The Lodge, which has changed little in appearance over the years, is a three-storey, castellated, residential property inhabited by David Bewer and family.

When used as the Fort "mess" at the turn of the century, it consisted of basement, ground floor lavatory, kitchen, larder, scullery and Drawing and Dining rooms, in addition to four bedrooms and a bathroom on the first floor. Above the staircase on the second floor were the servants' quarters.

Landguard Lodge in Manor Terrace
Officers Mess. 1890's

The main part of the Lodge appears to have been linked, by a covered passageway, to an additional wing which may have housed more servants.

The following account was written by Lieutenant F. S. Yorke, who was stationed at Landguard Fort in 1905, when the Lodge Mess was combined R. A. and R. E., and "the corps" was represented by a Submarine Mining Company.

This unit, in addition to Lights, ran the minefield and the dirigible Brennan Torpedo in the harbour mouth. (The Brennan Torpedo was invented by Louis Brennan and adopted in 1887 by the War Office as a harbour defence weapon. It was said to be able to hit almost any small floating object at

17

two thousand yards, and was capable of being turned through 180 degrees 'and so attack a ship from the offside.') The young Lieutenant recorded the fact that in 1905 Admiral Sir John Fisher had this form of warfare taken out of military hands.

Yorke had been posted to No. 12 Coy., Royal Garrison Artillery. He arrived at his destination late in the afternoon, having hired a horse-drawn cab from a rank outside Felixstowe Town Station.

Other than a man from the guard who managed to find the Orderly Sergeant and a gunner, who was to act as batman to the young commissioned officer, the fort appeared to be deserted.

Lieutenant, cab driver and newly-appointed batman struggled over the wooden drawbridge with several pieces of luggage, past coal stores, guardroom, and a second drawbridge leading to the inner Courtyard, from where a flight of stone steps led to the first floor balcony officers' quarters.

He was not too happy with these arrangements when he learned that other subalterns had been housed at the more comfortable Landguard Lodge.

One evening, while dressing for dinner, Yorke spotted what he later referred to as 'invaders of a very different kind.' Scorpions! Making a speedy exit from his room, he ran down the steps towards the outer courtyard and guardroom, to report what he had seen.

The warm kitchens had attracted even more of the insects! Apparently they were from a fruit-carrying cargo vessel which had broken up a short distance off the coast. Eggs laid in ships' timbers floating ashore had hatched out beneath a warm sun, resulting in the young scorpions being obliged to

18

seek out places offering conditions similar to those enjoyed in their natural habitat. Fortunately, they were quickly despatched - and no harm done!

Landguard Fort appears to have been extremely well fortified, and we have the young Lieutenant to thank for recording the following information.

'Starting at Beacon Hill and working across there was a 10-inch Breech Loading disappearing gun: Four 5-inch (practice battery) and four 12-pounders, all on the Harwich side.

'On Darell's Battery there were two 6-inch Breech Loaders, two 4-inch Quick Firing, two 12-pounders, two 6-inch MK VII and one 10-inch MK IV LCP.'

He also reported seeing 'a most extraordinary weapon' - the only one of its kind, apparently - an experimental mounting, a 10-inch gun on a MK V mounting, like an enormous 9.2-inch.

Then came two 6-inch MK II on slides and two 3-pounder Q. E., these last four being for practice only. There was also another 10-inch disappearing gun, its carriage known as the "Australian pattern" because Sydney Harbour had invested in this type of mounting.

To the left of this piece was an emplacement containing two 6-inch breech loading MK IV guns and one x 10-inch breech loading gun. It was named "Landguard Left Battery".

Below were shelters, shell, cartridge and artillery stores; lamp rooms, cartridge, fuze and dial recesses and a tank for two hundred gallons of water - the whole being linked by a maze of passages lit by lamps placed in recesses in the walls. Rumours of underground passages leading from Left and Right

Batteries to the fort interior, however, have not been proved.

In those days nearly all low-sited batteries were the disappearing type of mounting; the recoil lowered the gun, and the subsequent compression of the liquid in the cylinder raised it to the firing position when a valve was opened.

These guns were in the process of being removed from the fort interior by the time Lieutenant Yorke arrived. Both Darell's Battery and Landguard Right had been built, 'so putting most of those old monsters out of business.'

Yorke recorded a simple means of communication, which was to roll a written message in a hollow wooden ball, drop it into a cage, pull a wire and let it roll away, on a sort of aerial railway, to its appropriate group. Sending and reception headquarters was at the Fire Command Post (built on the roof-top close to King's Bastion).

One gun group commander, as he was then known, opened his ball, scribbled an acknowledgement, threw in half a crown, and added the words, 'take one eleven three.' His leave was stopped for a year!

Within the fort at the turn of the century was a tremendous armament. Each barrack room was the emplacement for a 10-inch rifled muzzle loading gun of 38 tons.

In the seaward bastions were the 12.5s; a larger edition of the 10-inch and weighing 45 tons. Although equipped with projectiles, these guns were mainly for "running past". Running past was a fine sport. Each 10-inch gun was loaded with a cylinder containing sixty 3½ lbs. chilled steel balls, the 12.5s with ninety. The guns were laid at a given range and bearing to cover certain channels, so that all possible approaches would be under fire.

By the old Fire Command Post was a firing post containing a gadget with arms corresponding to individual guns and groups of guns and laid on the prescribed area. Each arm had a fore and back sight and was laid with due regard to displacement from the group or gun it served.

When the targets dashed through the lighted area, the Observation Officer touched off the electric keys under each sight. The resulting phenomenon was magnificent and the effect appalling on the old type of torpedo boat, for the decks would have been swept clean. Unfortunately, it took a good three minutes before another round could be loaded.

Victorian casemated battery for seven rifled muzzle loaded guns. Built 1875. Note armour surrounding gun ports.

Photograph: Bunny Rayner

Massive vaulted ceilings in the Victorian casemated battery (barrack rooms where thick armour surrounds the gun port) contain hooks for side-arms and muzzle loading gear. It is still possible to see traces of the reversing arc. The back of each chamber is distinctive from the emplacement proper, and is where, in peacetime, the detachment slept on iron beds. At other times they slept in hammocks.

Inner Courtyard. Unaltered since the 1870's.

Photograph: Bunny Rayner

On practice days, the whole of the wooden back, or entrance, to chambers on the first floor balcony was removed to avoid breaking glass windows. The gun dials were between emplacements, and one long passage was made by removing the side doors, so that the gun group commanders could communicate. Each chamber accommodated between ten and sixteen, making a total of ninety-two men, while the six barrack rooms on the ground floor housed ten.

Years later, smaller chambers above were converted to (from left to right) Officers' toilets, barber's shop, post room, Fire Command clerk, Army Officers' clerk, Officers' servants, Officers' war or bomb-proof shelters, Court Martial room, and single Sergeants' Room.

Lieutenant Yorke ends an interesting account by referring to the enormous manning detail required in 1905, which included the regular Royal Garrison Artillery Company, the Norfolk Military Militia, and the Essex and Suffolk Volunteer Artillery. The Royal Engineers also had their own Militia and Volunteer quota, so there was plenty of personnel: a good two thousand gunners at least on mobilisation.

FIRE COMMAND POST

In 1904, a Fire Command Post was built on top of the fort roof, close to King's bastion and above the 1875 casemated battery for seven guns. It was an L-shaped building with concrete floors, its walls supporting a concrete roof topped with steel corrugated roof plate. The interior included an observing cell and telephone room.

In the early nineteen thirties this was known as the Chief Battery Command Post, the name being changed to Gunnery Control during the 1939/45 war.

By 1915, a Naval Signal Station with accommodation for signal crew appears to have taken over King's bastion. Work commenced on conversion in October of 1914 and was completed in February of the following year. Costs involved amounted to four hundred and twenty-five pounds.

The former bastion became a Chief Officers' room, and

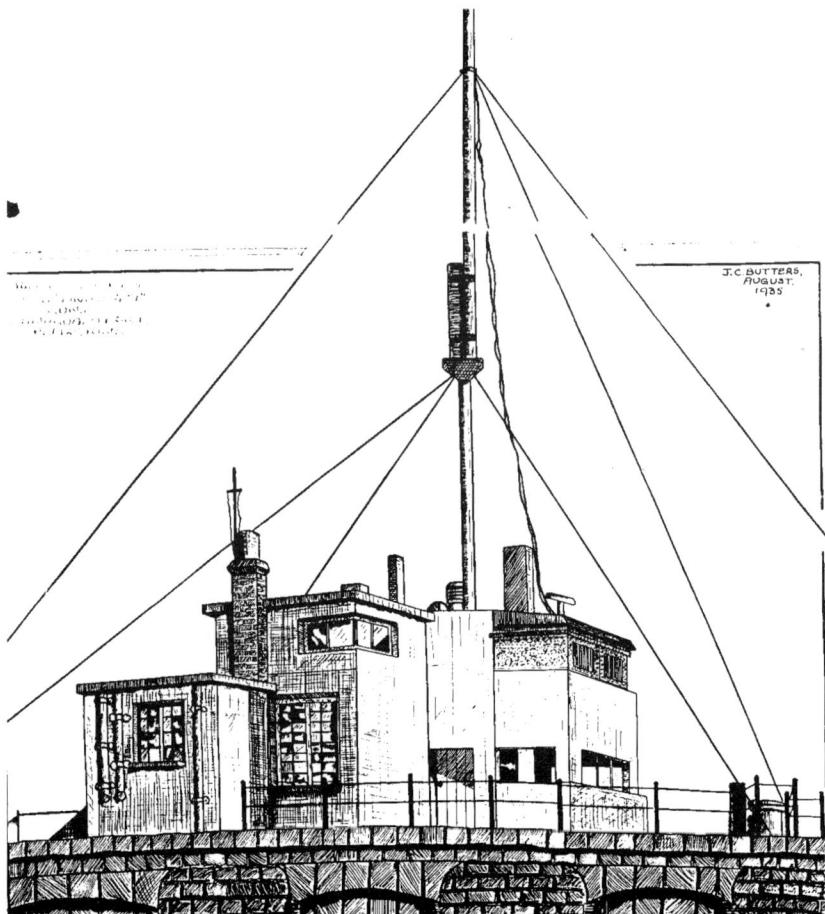

The old Fire Command Post (1904) Battery Command Post (1933) for two 6-inch and 4.7-inch guns and Gunnery Control 1935.

Drawing by the young John Butters (August 1935)

adjoining that was a cookhouse, or small kitchen, which led into the mess and also to sleeping quarters. The concrete floor of each chamber was covered with floorboards, and a heating stove was installed. Hammock hooks left set into the walls following demolition of the signal station may still be seen; the area being included in guided tours of the fort interior.

Landguard Football Team 1904
with Landguard Cup.
Ipswich and District League
(now Suffolk and Ipswich Football League)

Names of players.
H.Rose (Captain) seated
From Left to Right.
J. Doughty, W. Green, A. Moore, A. Peacock
E. Ryan, C. Hinds, W. Heard, J. Shaw, W. Flecknoe and A. Elwin.

Photograph courtesy of John Smith, Felixstowe.

Main entrance to fort C1910
Left to right, surnames only.
G.Dodd, Brown, child, Burley, Pryke, Laurence, Dungarrar.

SIXTH SUFFOLK CYCLISTS COOK HOUSE.
LANDGUARD SEPTR 1911.

Sixth Suffolk Cyclists Cook House.
Landguard. September 1911

PASS. No. 3476

This Pass is not transferable and must be returned on Expiry to the Provost Marshal, at address below.

Name *Mr S. b. Wall*

Address *High St, Walton*

has permission until 31 May, 1915, to pass

Walton — Lower Walton

between the hours of *nine* a.m. and *seven* p.m.

for the purpose of *Watchmaker etc*

Town Hall, Felixstowe.

Captain,
A.P.M.,
Harwich Garrison.

Date 6/5 1915.

O.P. 3.—1800—23.4.15.—J. C. & Co.

Owner to sign here *Wall*

Air Raid Damage, Felixstowe. 22.7.17.

Garrison Lane

27

FIRST WORLD WAR.

In August of 1914, the appropriate authorities prepared to defend Felixstowe by bringing a large military force into the district. Busy and exciting scenes were reported at the town station during the afternoon of the 11th, when the Territorials began to occupy a potentially dangerous coastal area as entire families moved out.

By late evening the town was under military control, with members of the public being forbidden access to the seafront, where lights had been extinguished at an earlier than usual hour.

The Bedfords were encamped in wooden huts on Landguard Common, the Norfolks in Mill Lane, the North Lancashire Regiment in Brook Lane, and the Suffolks in an area we know today as St. Andrew's Road. They were all bound for France and Belgium.

An *East Anglian Daily Times* newspaper report headed Patriotic Felixstowe Citizens, applauded uncomplaining residents who had either evacuated home, or given up at least one downstairs room, as requested by the military.

Felixstowe and Walton had become Special Military Areas and, in 1915, passes were issued, as per No. 3476 made out in the name of Mr. S. D. Wall (local historian 1880-1977).

By 1916, anyone wishing to enter or leave the district was forced to carry permit books, to be shown to sentries posted at various barriers, such as those placed on the Trimley High Road or Town Station. Beaches were mined and cordoned off with barbed wire, and trenches dug alongside

Air Raid damage to Blacksmith Shop, Old Felixstowe 22-07-17

Air Raid damage to The Ordnance Hotel, Felixstowe 22-07-17
Civilians were killed here.

Note: In this daylight raid on the Harwich area a total of 55 bombs were dropped, 13 people were killed and 26 injured.

On the 17th June 1917, Zeppelin L48 was shot down by Lt. L.P.Watkins of 37 Squadron, in a B.E.12 flying from Goldhanger. The Zeppelin came down at Holly Tree Farm, near Theberton, close to the Admiralty intercept station.

Three of the crew survived and were taken prisoner. The remainder including the commander Kapitänleutnant Franz Eichler are buried in the German War Cemetery at Cannock Chase.

the promenade.

Leaflets headed *Instructions For the Guidance of the Civil Population in the event of a Landing by the Enemy on the Coast* were issued to local residents who had refused to move out of town. The leaflets not only advised of action to be taken if an hostile enemy force landed on the beach, but also pointed out that items must be removed inland, rendered useless, or destroyed by owners (to include all forms of transport, petrol, livestock and other foodstuffs) as and when ordered to do so.

Main roads were to be kept clear for troop movement, pedestrians or cyclists being the exception. Because railways were under the control of the military authorities, they would not be available for evacuation purposes. Residents of both towns were warned that at a moments notice they may be ordered to leave their homes and the area, provision having already been made for the sick and infirm. Failure to comply with any or all of these instructions would result in loss of compensation!

Most air raids took place at night, but early in the morning of June 17th, 1917, Zeppelin L.48 crashed in flames at Theberton, after making repeated unsuccessful attempts to bomb Landguard Fort and the Air Station.

Samuel D. Wall recorded a daylight raid on Wednesday, 4th July, 1917, when he counted ten enemy aircraft over the town, and another on Sunday, July 22nd, in which several residents were killed, including some working at the Air Station. It was during the latter raid that the blacksmith's shop at Old Felixstowe was demolished and houses were damaged on the High Road and in Garrison Lane.

Another newspaper report, dated June 18th, 1917, mentions a raid carried out by two enemy airships. One crossed

31

the Kentish coast at about 2 a.m. and dropped six bombs on a coast town. A large number of houses were damaged, sixteen people were injured, and two killed.

The second raider, which attacked Felixstowe at about 2.30 a.m., was heavily shelled by anti aircraft guns and driven away.

The airship, thought to have been damaged by local gunfire, made off towards Kirton, where it dropped a number of bombs. Fortunately, they fell on open land, so that there were neither casualties nor damage to property. At Theberton, it was engaged by a pilot of the Royal Flying Corps, and brought down in flames.

Little appears to have been recorded regarding Landguard Fort during the 1914/18 war. It was occupied by The Royal Artillery, Royal Engineers and the Suffolk Regiment, but is thought to have been relatively quiet, guns being seldom used.

1st W.W. Mortar Gun Crew, Landguard Common.

"C" COMPANY 4TH VOLUNTEER BATTALION, SUFFOLK REGIMENT, DECEMBER 1918

Men named were from Walton or Felixstowe.

4th row, standing.
Second left: J. Ward, Builder.
Third left: W. W. Coways, Chemist.

3rd row, seated.
Second left: ? Randall. Occupation unknown.

Second row, seated.
Sixth right: ?Bunting, Grocer.
Fifth right: A. W. Potter.
Fourth right: H. F. Douthwaite, Chemist.

First row, seated.
Third left: E. E. Burt, Grocer.
Eighth left: Haylett Horner, Banker.
Eighth right: C. D. Phillips, Stationer.
Fifth right: ? Downay, Outfitter.
Seated. First row, second right: ? Jacobs.

Those sitting on ground remain unknown.

Photograph and names' list courtesy of Mr. D. Burt of Felixstowe, retired Grocer.

Charles Willis was head foreman of the Army Ordnance Depot at Harwich, in Essex. He worked at the Depot for almost forty years and lived at Ordnance House with his wife and twelve children. His duties during the 1914/18 war entailed supplying armaments to Beacon Hill fort, Shotley Barracks and Landguard Fort. Mr. Willis used a government pinnace boat to reach all three places.

The naval base at Harwich supported British, American and Italian fleets. There were also ships stationed at Landguard Point - rather like mine sweepers - which were called "gate ships". These were designed to guard against enemy submarines entering the harbour.

Ordnance House was approximately two hundred yards from the esplanade, so the children saw much of the naval vessels going to battle in the North Sea. Often these ships returned home with great holes in their sides and carrying the dead and wounded.

During a 3.00 a.m. Zeppelin raid, Harwich residents watching from their windows saw the searchlights from the forts at Felixstowe and Harwich latch on to "a large silver cigar", which burst into flames when it was shot down over Landguard. On that same night, a bomb landing in Government House gardens failed to explode!

Charles Willis retired as head foreman in 1919, when the Ordnance Depot closed down. The troops were withdrawn from Landguard and Harwich a few years later. Sadly, Ordnance House received a direct hit in World War II and was completely demolished.

During the 1920s, one of the Willis girls worked in the NAAFI at the Royal Air Force Station, Felixstowe. At that time, the pilots of flying boats, namely Squadron Leader A.H.

Orlebar and Flight Lieutenants N. Webster, G.H. Stainforth, D'Arcy, Greig and R.L.R. Atcherley, trained for the Schneider Trophy race over Southampton waters, later winning the Trophy for Britain.

Mary Willis (who became Mrs. Mary Rutley) recalled the arrival of L. A. C. Shaw, alias Lawrence of Arabia. 'He was,' she wrote, 'a rather timid man who preferred his own company, declining to live in the Officers' Mess or to eat with colleagues. He made it very clear to everyone that he simply wanted a quiet rest without fuss or question before going abroad. He was nothing like the man portrayed by Peter O'Toole in the film *Lawrence of Arabia*.

Royal Naval Air Station, Felixstowe.
Runners up, Garrison Cup 1915/16
Names unknown

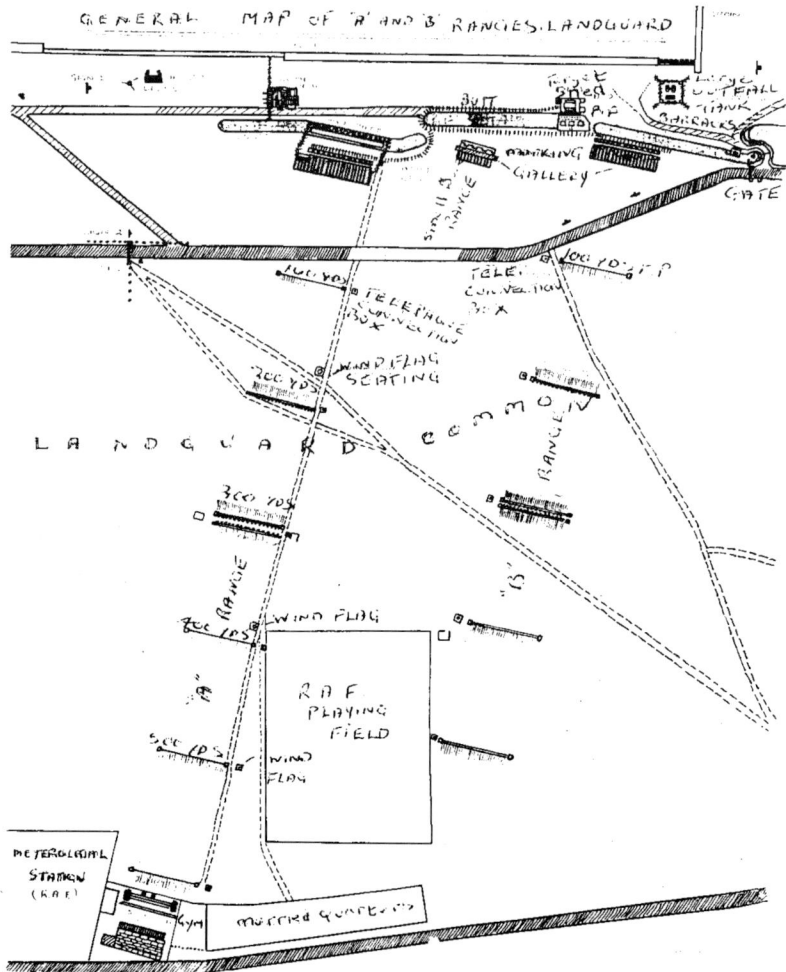

General map of A and B ranges, Landguard

RIFLE RANGES.

My appeal for information relating to Landguard Fort and peninsular resulted in a meeting with John Butters, a retired Architect living at Ipswich, who furnished the writer with much interesting information relating to Landguard during the 1920s and 1930s. Long ago pencilled notes and drawings made by the then thirteen-year-old boy have been included within the following pages.

There was often practice firing at Brackenbury and Landguard Forts and at Harwich during the 1920s, but the biggest and loudest guns were the 9-inch at Brackenbury.

The object was to hit square targets towed by tugs approximately two miles from the shore. While this exercise was taking place, a red flag indicating "danger" would be raised on a tall mast for all to see, while a patrolman on a bicycle made certain that access to the Point was barred.

The crack of rifle shots would echo across the common, as grey and buff targets in front of the butts mysteriously appeared from out of the ground, only to disappear back into it within a matter of seconds.

During this period, there was also much activity in the air; many types of seaplane and flying boat were based at Felixstowe R.A.F. station, which was established before the 1914/18 war. The Schneider Trophy seaplanes were being tested there in the 1920s, and townsfolk and day trippers soon became accustomed to the noise they made. Whenever the weather was favourable, the aeroplanes would drone overhead, taking off and landing on the harbour and returning to moorings near the old Station Pier. Even the largest flying boat could be lifted out of the water by a huge gantry crane at the R.A.F. jetty.

High speed rescue launches with aero engines demonstrated their superiority over naval cutters, often going to sea in rough weather. The prototype Sunderland, was also tested at Felixstowe.

Entering and leaving the harbour and passing close to Landguard Point were "regulars", such as the Danish butter boats in grey, black and red livery; the *Kronprinz Frederick* and the *Esberg* bringing dairy produce. Danish bacon was part of the English traditional breakfast in those days, and this is where it arrived - at Felixstowe!

The stop butts, which appeared rather like sloping cliffs, just south of Landguard Lodge in Manor Terrace, were man-made and were ingeniously angled to absorb bullets from three firing ranges laid out across the common.

Close behind the first of these mounds, stood (previously mentioned) South House, a forbidding dwelling with grey rendered, pock-marked walls, a slate roof, windows covered with thick steel plates, and a front door facing north. It predated the rifle ranges, and consequently became uninhabitable when these were built, although, as a store, it remained useful to the Royal Engineers.

A little further on was the Target Workshop, a large, steel-framed building with roof lights and clad in corrugated iron. Narrow gauge, light railway tracks emerged from its doorway and ran along the side of the butts to markers' galleries on the other side.

Immediately above the workshop, and affording it better

Musketry Office converted to target shed.

Drawing of interior. John Butters September 1935

protection from stray bullets, was a higher section of embankment in which were embedded various brick and concrete lookout posts, facing seawards. These Position Firing posts were for taking bearings on approaching vessels, and had been used to co-ordinate all three batteries. The stop butts terminated at the Fort entrance.

Just past the 6-inch battery stood a Victorian bungalow inhabited by the civilian Warden. It is still there and, at the time of writing, has became a base and offices for the Landguard Warden.

Camouflaged Searchlight Post.

Drawing by John Butters, August 1935

There were gratings in the ground above a huge nearby underground sewage outfall tank, (the fort complex having no treatment plant) and a two-storey searchlight post, "ludicrously camouflaged with paint", which could be easily spotted by approaching enemy aircraft.

There was also a small jetty, about one hundred and fifty yards long, projecting from the Point and visible from all parts of the Felixstowe seafront.

The massive emplacements (Left and Right Batteries) were for 6-inch coastal defence guns and, although well fenced in, one clearly sees the whole arrangement of galleries, workshops, crew rooms, and magazines with the gun turrets on top, just protruding above the embankment and pointing out to sea.

Right Battery 1930's

From a drawing by John Butters

There was a gravel beach on this side and, when the guns were to be fired, "unsinkable" rafts, carrying targets, were brought out of the Fort and drawn up nearby, in readiness. Beyond the Fort boundary was another high fence, enclosing the R.A.F. station.

Concerning Callender's

TIDE INDICATOR AT FELIXSTOWE

For the benefit of shipping using Harwich Harbour, the Conservancy Board have lately erected an automatic tide gauge and indicator that is unique. It is situated on the Felixstowe side near Languard Fort, and tidal readings are visible on both sides from any part of the Harbour and Harwich Quays.

As our photograph shows, the indicator is a heavy steel structure, specially strengthened to withstand gale conditions ; it is 30 ft. high and has a clock face with a dial of 10-ft. diameter. Special marks and radial arms represent the numerals and " hands " respectively, these being fitted with neon tubes and illuminated throughout day and night. The automatic actuating gear is operated by a float and balance weight from the building on the jetty. The light tubes change with every foot rise and fall of the tide.

Messrs. W. Simms & Co., Ltd., of Felixstowe, were responsible for all the electrical work and used our materials throughout ; in addition to overhead equipment we supplied a special 18-core L.S.S.W.A. compound rubber insulated cable for the " clock " actuating circuits.

An unique, automatic tide gauge, erected by the Harwich Harbour Conservancy Board in the 1930s, gave tidal readings visible far out to sea and from within the harbour. It was thirty feet high, had a ten feet diameter dial with numerals and hands similar to a clock face, and was fitted with neon tubes lit day and night. With every foot rise or fall of the tide, the light tubes changed. John recalled this being an outstanding sight at night, both from land and the sea, over which it cast an eerie light.

The route back to Manor Road lay through lines of single-storey barracks and across the rifle range. The thirteen-year-old enthusiast was always amazed that his frequent appearances on Landguard Common, with camera, binoculars, sketch pad and pencils, was never questioned by the military, even though it was a War Department base. This fact may well have been due, of course, to the recognised apprentice/tradesman relationship which had developed between himself and the range Warden, Harry Vines.

THE LURE OF LANDGUARD. 1920s/1930s.

During the nineteen twenties and thirties, only one of the rifle ranges, that closest to Felixstowe town, was in use. However, it was still possible to see the 1914 layout, which would have allowed hundreds of soldiers to practice each day. Ranges were laid out on NW-SE parallel axes between Landguard Lodge and the Fort, and extended back to the boundary of the Royal Air Force station, just over six hundred yards distant. The ground being flat, it had been necessary, for safety at sea, to construct artificial stop butts about 30 feet high, close behind the sea wall on the east side of the common.

There were three of these, the north butt having South House hard up against its "safe" side, its roof and chimneys visible over the top and only yards from the line of fire; the centre butt, which had originally served a small bore and pistol range, and incorporated a group of P. F. (position firing) posts looking seawards, for artillery ranging; and the south butt, a replica of the north butt, linking the P. F. posts with the earthworks guarding the Fort entrance.

Each range had a marker's gallery positioned close behind its stop butt, which provided the setting for steel-framed target frames. The north and south galleries had twelve sets of these frames, each carrying pairs of targets in a counterbalancing arrangement, with chains and pulleys. These were pulled down manually, so that there was always one up and one down.

The men's comfort was not overlooked. They could be on duty in the gallery for several hours at a time, and each man had a seat, coat peg and small recess in the back wall for his sandwich pack.

There were separate latrines for Officers and men, and a cupboard for a field telephone in the centre of the range for targets. The light railway line already mentioned ran parallel to the brick trench, for convenient handling of targets.

The north range was six hundred yards long, its six firing points being laid out across the grassed Common, 100 yards apart and parallel to the stop butt. At 100, 400, 500 and 600 yards, there were just low banks where men could stand, kneel, or adopt the prone position, for firing. At 200 hundred yards there was a higher embankment, behind which marksmen could stand, half concealed, or climb over and fire from the parapet, crouched or prone.

The 300 yard point had a timber-lined trench, designed

44

for firing from fire steps. Each position had a field telephone box in a manhole, and there were three settings across the range for a wind direction flag.

The range was administered by the Officer Commanding Troops, Harwich Garrison. From him The Felixstowe Rifle Club, a civilian body, obtained permission to use it for their practice shoots, every Saturday afternoon, from May to September. Up to 1933, it was also the venue for the Suffolk County Rifle Association annual shoot, an event encouraging competition between all three armed services in the region and expert civilian marksmen. It was the busiest day of the year on the range, and the results determined who should represent Suffolk at Bisley. Some civilians were 1914/1918 veterans.

Many families and unaccompanied children would walk towards the common and see a red flag (to indicate shooting in progress) flying near Landguard Lodge, and the gate across Landguard Road closed. There was usually a lone sentry on duty, with perhaps 300 yards to patrol, and no fence.

The sentry was often a teenage boy (JB), hoping to double his pocket money, and his instructions were to prevent anyone proceeding along the beach, or towards the butts, whilst shooting was in progress. He was also required to deal with frustrated motorists, their way to the common blocked by a single bar gate, and to keep an eye seawards in case any boat approached close behind the butts.

If any of these rules were broken, the flag had to be lowered and shooting would cease until the area was clear. Most people co-operated, but some resented the restrictions, and demanded of a young civilian sentry that he show written proof of authority.

Left: Harry Vines, Landguard Warden at Landguard, 1934.

Below: Floating Targets. The beach at Landguard Point, 1934

THE RANGE WARDEN

Range Warden Harry Vines and twelve-year-old John Butters met one Saturday afternoon in the early 1930s, during a summer shooting season when the Felixstowe Rifle Club had use of the range.

Part of the warden's job was to care for "all the paraphernalia" required for operating a .303 in battle practice range, a great deal of this work being carried out in his workshop behind the butts.

Harry was an ex regular soldier, a "civilian subordinate", to quote the unfortunate official military phrase of those days, when he and others like him were given preference in work which could he done by trusted civilians in War Office establishments. He lived in Seckford Street, Woodbridge, and every day, whatever the weather, cycled thirteen miles to his workplace at Landguard Fort.

Preparations for a shoot included loading up one or two railway trolleys with up to 12 targets, two field telephones, marking and spotting discs, various flags, pots of paste, coloured paper for running repairs, the keys and duty board.

When the RAF personnel who were to operate the targets arrived, the warden would depart to the southern flagstaff, by the Fort, to hoist the red flag and take up his pistol. Heavy truckloads of gear would be pushed along the railway tracks about 300 yards to the markers gallery. The targets would then be unloaded and placed in counterbalanced frames. At the end of a shoot, when marksmen telephoned they had finished, (from the 600 yard firing point) all the gear had to be loaded back onto trolleys and pushed round the butts to the workshop.

The Warden had some additional help, in the form of Fred Gorham, who lived at Walton. He was a middle-aged white-haired man with a ruddy complexion who dressed in black striped trousers, black jacket and bowler hat. He and Harry worked well together, looking after the Fort and Common prior to the 1939/45 war.

Landguard was an ideal viewing platform whilst the latest version of the design for the Schneider Trophy Races was put through its paces. It was never completely quiet at the military end of town.

The sea and the wind; the sounds of flying boats and aero engines on test beds near to the Hangers could, John recalled, be heard as far away as the Town Station.

There was some consternation, early in 1939, when the Graf Zeppelin appeared, flying northwards up the coast, less than one thousand feet in the air. It was later discovered that the airship was carrying special monitoring equipment to verify the existence of British radar transmissions. As it happened, the new radar system was switched on and tracking the Zeppelin.

There was also talk of a death ray being developed at Bawdsey, the rumour spreading when a flying boat operating close to the Cork Lightship crashed into the sea with loss of crew. John remembers watching the incident through binoculars as the wreckage was hoisted from the sea-bed and brought ashore to Landguard Point. War was not far away.

GUNS AND GUN CREWS. 1940.

The manning of coastal defence guns at the outbreak of the second world war was a Territorial Army function. Relevant units were the Suffolk Heavy Regiment, Royal

January 1940.
A bleak winter when water pipes became frozen.

Artillery (R.A.) - composed of 166th and 167th Batteries -
and the Royal Engineers.

During the first six months of the 1939/45 war, the
original members of 166th Battery at Landguard Fort were
supplemented by two, additional detachments. The first was
from the 67th Medium Regiment, R.A. (T.A.) at Ipswich. This
detachment consisted of gunners who were under the age of
nineteen and, therefore, (under the legislation of the time) not
allowed to be sent overseas. They were labelled "Immatures".

The second detachment, arriving early in 1940, were from
the first batch of militia, who had been called up in the summer
of 1939, at the age of twenty, for compulsory military service
and who had completed their basic army training.

Right Battery at Landguard (1940) consisted of two 6-inch Mk VII guns with a maximum range of about 18,000 yards. Each emplacement was made up of a concrete platform with a waist-high parapet at the front.

The gun crew consisted of about ten men - the gun sergeant, the breech operator, two loading numbers, the gun-layer (controlling the elevation), the bearing operator, and four ammunition handlers.

Gun crews were never further away than the shelters next to the guns. There was always a lookout at the Command Post and at each gun.

Interior chamber of Victorian Gun Battery.
Left to right: Len Parker, Corporal 'Dinkie' Ward and Sergeant Webber. 1940

Darell's Battery consisted of two 4.7-inch guns mounted on a pedestal bolted to the floor of a pit about six feet deep. Each gun had a maximum range of about 10,000 yards, and its crew consisted of eight men, who were always nearby throughout the night - the most likely time for an E-boat attack. Searchlights were always manned, ready for use from dawn to dusk, with the generators for them running all night.

Gun crews were divided into five watches, each of which had a five day cycle of duties - each 24-hour duty starting at midday.
an example:

(a)   Reserve duties for Darell's Battery.
      Duty started with the midday meal on the first day and ended with the midday meal on the second day. During the day, the watch was employed on various fatigues (cookhouse, cleaning etc.); during the night, the watch slept in its own quarters, unless there was an alarm.

(b)   Duty on Right Battery (highest standard of readiness). The whole 24 hours were spent on, or near to, the guns, supper or breakfast being brought to the gun shelters. The day was spent on training or cleaning and maintenance at the guns; evening hours were spent in the shelters, undergoing oral instruction by the gun sergeant; the rest of the night was spent cat-napping, fully dressed! Each member of the crew spent one hour on lookout duty throughout the 24 hours.

(c)   Reserve duties on Right Battery started with the midday meal on the third day and ended with the midday meal on the fourth day. Daylight hours were spent on training and instruction, with an hour or so on the "dummy loader", practising loading one minute spells at rates up to 15 or so rounds a minute. Supper and breakfast were taken in the mess hall.

The winter of 1940 was so severe that the one hour lookout period was reduced to 30 minutes, and braziers had to be placed by the guns, to prevent the oil in the recoil system from solidifying.

In the spring of 1940, two 12-pounder guns were installed in Darell's Battery, alongside the two 4.7-inch guns. The latter were later dismounted and sent off to be part of the coast defence installation at Narvik during the Norwegian campaign.

Later still, two twin 6-pounders were installed, and the 12-pounders removed. The twin 6-pounders were traversed and elevated in unison from a control position situated at the top of a 25 feet concrete tower near to the gun mounting. Twin towers still exist today.

Manor House Battery was an emergency gun battery. Two ex naval 6-inch guns were mounted in beach emplacements. The Battery Command Post was in the Manor House itself. Troops were accommodated in nearby evacuated houses.

After the end of World War II, the coast defences at Landguard Fort were placed on to a care and maintenance basis. In 1956, it was decided the effectiveness of air power, coupled with the advent of guided missiles, had rendered the fixed coastal defence artillery concept obsolete. Therefore, guns and other equipment at all coast defence installations were removed.

The main fort building was used for a while as barrack accommodation, but the subsidiary buildings etcetera to the north and west of the fort were eventually demolished, as the Container Port grew. The fort was then left empty and neglected until the Felixstowe History and Museum Society successfully drew attention to its importance as part of the country's historical heritage.

A. R. CLARK, of Lytham St. Anne's, spent a month at Landguard Fort in 1938, whilst serving with the R. O. A. C. He had recently qualified as an Ammunitions Examiner and was given the task of inspecting and testing 6-inch gun cartridges which were nearing the end of their shelf life. At that time, there was a military jetty within the fort complex from where heavy items of ordnance could be transported by sea and unloaded on the doorstep. It was not actually used for this purpose during his stay, but he admits to spending many hours on the jetty, enjoying what was virtually private fishing.

'Fish was more plentiful in those days and I recall catching cod, sole, and Jarfish by rod and line, and lobsters by nets dropped over the end of the jetty.'

Ghost stories abounded. Some insisted footsteps could be plainly heard when there was no one about to make them. Others claimed to have seen the ghosts of Nathaniel Darell (Governor from 1667-1670) and the Earl of Holland (Governor from 1628-1649), the latter riding a white horse! Ghostly footsteps were explained away as being nothing more than the sound of halliards flapping against the flag mast when the wind blew in a certain direction.

In addition are stories of sentries, Quartermasters and Army schoolmasters committing suicide at this bleak outpost.

One (1992) Sunday, while conducting a group around the fort interior, the author was handed a copy of a February 15th, 1924, edition of the *East Anglian Daily Times* newspaper. It was headed 'Tragic Discovery at Landguard' and informed readers of the shooting of a Quarter Master-Sergeant. He was about 40 years of age, had been married for approximately eighteen months, and was due to be discharged at the end of the year.

In 1938, The Royal Air Force used the waters just off the shore as a flying boat base, and there was usually a line of moored boats about two hundred yards out. The upper section of the Mayo Composite aircraft crashed into the Stour, just off the fort, during trials.

While at Landguard, my informant made the acquaintance of a young gunner who was willing to show him how the larger guns worked.

Compressed air was used to move the guns about and to operate the ammunition hoists etc. By the time the demonstration was completed, the pressure of the stored air had dropped a little. Unfortunately, the pair had been observed by the Battery Sergeant Major, who insisted they top up the pressure again, not by using the electric pumps, but by use of an emergency hand pump which was designed to be operated by six or eight men! It took some time and a lot of hard work before their tormentor declared himself satisfied!

BALLOON BUSTERS.

FRANK GLOVER, of Ipswich, related an amusing incident involving his gun team, members of which were ever afterwards referred to as "the balloon busters".

Motor Torpedo Boats from Harwich regularly went out on nightly patrols in the North Sea, seeking enemy shipping and the E-boats which protected them. International law insisted that all MTBs re-entering Harwich must stop for interrogation by a Naval Examination Vessel, which was anchored about fifteen hundred yards from the shore.

The strict order was usually complied with .... until the day when seven MTBs arrived back to base at the same time. They were a most impressive sight, with their bows held high out of the sea, water cascading along the hulls. All was not well, however, for they refused to obey the command to STOP, whereby Frank's team received the signal from Exam. to go through the "bring to" procedure, by firing a warning shot across the bows of the leading vessel.

The command was given to number one gun to take post, at which the crew clambered up onto the gun platform. Additional commands were given in quick succession.

'Plug round. Load. Target, 1,000 yards, moving right. On target. Fire.'

There was a huge explosion, as the shell went straight over the top of a barrage balloon, which was being manually staked out and secured to the ground by Royal Air Force personnel. The ground crew fled in all directions, as the balloon suddenly burst into flames, with torches of fire falling everywhere. The shell landed a few yards in front of the leading MTB, so that they all found brakes and pulled up as one.

The friction of the shell passing over the balloon had ignited it - not impact, as at first suspected. Although the newly named "balloon busters" laughed for days over the episode, RAF personnel were definitely not amused.

During the second world war, Reserve Units lodged in the rifle range hut (demolished 1982), in Nissen huts situated in the ditch surrounding the fort, or in one of the sparsely furnished ground floor barrack rooms within the walls of the fort proper.

Bedding consisted of two blankets apiece, thrown onto the floor wherever men happened to be. Frank recalled it being so cold that men often slept in pairs, using one blanket as a ground sheet and three for warmth.

'We had the same blankets for nine months and they were filthy. God knows who used them before us, or when they were finally replaced.'

A rum ration, issued to the men every fifth day, was eagerly awaited and greatly appreciated!

On Parade.
Inner Courtyard
Landguard Fort.
May 5th 1940.

Photograph
courtesy of:
Mr. N.E.Pyman,
Grassmere Close,
Ipswich.

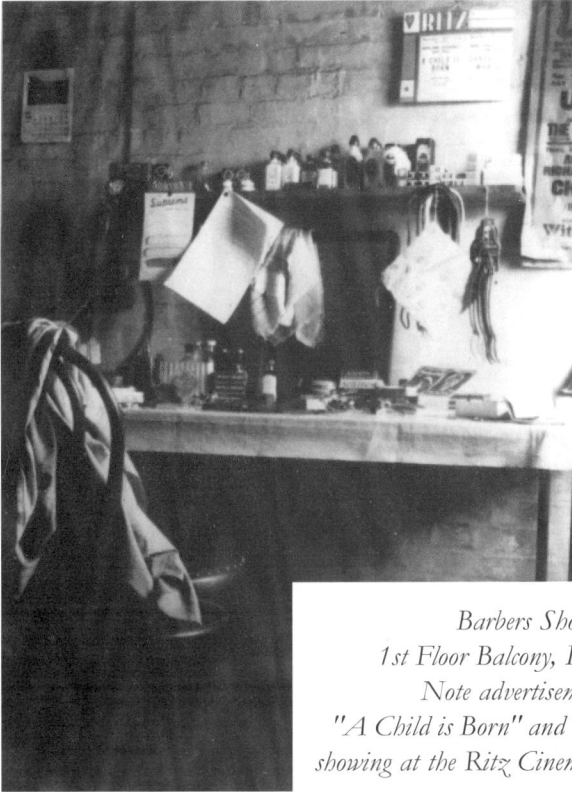

Barbers Shop 1940
1st Floor Balcony, Inner Courtyard.
Note advertisement on wall
"A Child is Born" and "Grapes of Wrath",
showing at the Ritz Cinema in Hamilton Road.

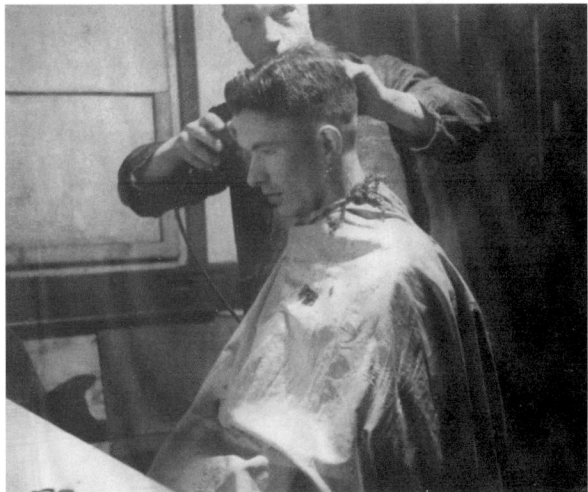

Photographs
courtesy of
J. Long,
Felixstowe.

BILL BURGOYNE was called up for military service on 12th December, 1940. He was posted to Landguard Battery in February of 1941, where he remained until August of that same year.

He and his pals usually spent two evenings per week in town, often visiting the Ritz Cinema, for one shilling, this treat to be followed by a sausages, chips and coffee supper for two shillings.

'If we did not have the necessary we settled for beans on toast and a mug of tea at the Y.M.C.A.'

Early in 1940, Lord Haw Haw, on German radio, referred to Landguard as "Hell Fire Corner", for a very warm reception awaited the enemy whenever they visited the area. Felixstowe beaches had been obstructed with large slabs of concrete down to the lowest point at low tide. These precautions were accompanied by barbed wire and strange frameworks of steel scaffolding, which, so it was rumoured, supported crude flame-throwers, to be used in the event of invasion.

A new road had also been built across Landguard Common, to accommodate military vehicles and equipment of all kinds.

The north side of the camp was bounded by several rows of barbed wire, which rolled right up to another fence of wire netting, and, 'there must have been more gun pits to the square inch than seen in any American movie.'

The 6-inch guns on which men served fired a shell weighing 105 lbs, which had to be loaded and rammed manually.

Service in France, Belgium, Holland and, finally,

Germany followed Bill Burgoyne's days at Landguard, and it was while serving in Germany that he and his comrades heard Sir Winston Churchill broadcasting the end of war in Europe.

In the summer of 1943, R.A.F. Felixstowe was a busy station under Coastal Command, operating High Speed Launches (H.S.L.s), with the motto, The Sea Shall Not Have Them.

Servicewomen such as Joan Rundle were often on duty when the boats were called out to rescue pilots who had been shot down. The Navy was also operating Motor Torpedo Boats (M.T.B.s) from the dock basin. Joan remembered the town as being very busy, with troops everywhere. There appeared to be plenty of places to go for entertainment: the seafront Cavendish Hotel (demolished 1987), with its regular mid-week and week-end dances, and the Ritz Cinema in Hamilton Road being amongst the most popular.

There was also "a very nice Tea Shop", which allowed servicewomen into the back parlour for a feast of special cakes and a glass of hot milk! They had to keep that quiet!

May and June of 1944 witnessed increasing numbers of troops appearing. It was the time of the proposed Normandy landings, an embarkation point being Landguard.

EXTRACTS FROM THE 1939/45 WAR DIARY
of:

ERNEST JOSEPH HILL, then of 8, Nacton Road, Felixstowe, a civilian employee at Felixstowe's Royal Air Force Seaplane Base from 1929 to 1955.

The diary was copied by his son, D. G. Hill, who later handed it into the care of The Felixstowe History and Museum Society.

A copy of the complete month by month diary is available for perusal, upon contact with the curator of the Felixstowe Museum.

Oct. 17th, 1939, Tuesday. Air raid. One machine over. No bombs dropped. Guns fired at same. Saw shells bursting all round.

Nov. 21st, 1939, Tuesday night. 9.20pm. H.M.S. *Gipsy* sunk in mouth of harbour by mine. I picked up about nine life jackets on the sea front on Wednesday morning.
(Note: compass box on display in Felixstowe Museum.)

Nov. 22nd, 1939, Wednesday. Anti aircraft guns on Landguard Common fired at machine over Manor House way about 1.25pm, as I was coming back from dinner. I stopped but could not see any enemy aircraft, only one of ours passed over Carr Road very low.

May 21st, 1940, Tuesday. Enemy aircraft over Manor House way at 12.30am. Dropped five bombs in the sea. Several windows smashed in the Manor House by explosion, but no other damage done. I was in bed when bombs dropped. They woke me up and I sat on the bed and looked out of the window but could not see any planes - only searchlights up.

June 12th, 1940, Wednesday. Firing at aircraft about 11.30pm. At about 3.00am one of our planes hit barrage balloon and fell on Marriage's mill and set it on fire. Four men were hurt - D. Grayling died in Cottage Hospital at 9.05pm Thursday night, from burns received. (see Note A)

June 18th, 1940, Thursday. At 11.30pm, heavy gun fire all round. I saw several enemy aircraft picked up in searchlights. Saw one machine come down in flames in sea in front of Hermen de Stern. Bombs were dropped but not near. Side-car and motor bike burnt out on Langer Road. (see Note B)

August 19th, 1940, Thursday. Bombs dropped near Town Station, Police Station and Council Yard. No one hurt. 3.00am, incendiary bombs dropped at Air Station also high explosive bombs fell in harbour. No damage done. At 9.00pm incendiary bomb fell on Pier Pavilion and went through roof. No one hurt.

Sept. 4th, 1940, Wednesday. Raid started 8.40pm. Bombs dropped in yacht pond and back of Percy House, Sea Road. Also Chaucer Road and Mill Lane. Windows in shops in Granville Road smashed. I went in my dug-out with wife, Sheila, Mrs. West and Mr. Mayes.

Sept. 18th, 1940, Wednesday. About 2.00am incendiary bombs dropped on Sergeants' Mess, Landguard Fort, and set it on fire. No gun fire.

Oct. 2nd, 1940, Wednesday. About 10.15am heard machine gun fire over No.1 Shed. Saw enemy bomber being chased by our fighters which was machine-gunning same. Bomber went out Ipswich way. One o'clock news reported, "Enemy bomber brought down in flames near Earl Soham." I expect this was the one. (I heard so later). (see Note C)

Oct. 12th, 1940, Saturday. Enemy plane over harbour. Guns at Landguard blazed at same - about 8 rounds. No bombs dropped.

Nov. 7th, 1940, Thursday. About 3.00 o'clock two enemy planes over Air Station. Machine gunned balloons and dropped 4 bombs - one on rails at Landguard boundary fence and 3 in sea. No one hurt.

Nov. 17th, 1940, Sunday. About 9.15am eight enemy planes over. Dropped bombs at back of dock cottages, one on dug-out, and demolished old school building in R.A.F. yard. One on married quarters compound near the meat hut. Windows broken and tiles on roof all out of place. One soldier killed at Dock, no one hurt at Air Station. 3 Boom Defence workers wounded. Young Minter was one of them and C. Phillips died in Cottage Hospital of wounds received.

Feb. 16th, 1941, Sunday. About 7.15pm enemy plane over. 2 bombs dropped back of dock cottages. No one hurt. Lot of gunfire. I was sitting by the fire with Sheila and it shook our old house some.

Feb. 24th, 1941, Wednesday. Siren went about 7.15pm. Lot of planes over. Flares dropped out to sea, no bombs dropped. It was my first night of fire watching. All Clear sounded at 11.00pm.

April 17th, 1941, Wednesday. Lot of enemy planes over all night. I was on fire watching duty until 5.00am. Biggest raid on London yet. No bombs dropped near. Plenty of gun fire.

May 12th, 1941. Monday morning. 3.00am. Bombs dropped in

Felixstowe Ferry, Bomb damage.

King Street, Walton, causing damage to houses and killing and injuring several people. Mrs. Lyon was killed and a soldier home on leave. Bombs dropped at several other points but no damage done. Lot of gunfire. Very bad night.

May 18th, 1941, Sunday. About 12.30am lot of gunfire out to sea. Planes dropped bombs Harwich way. Called up at 1.30am by Air Force to say water main burst at Landguard. I referred them to Mr. Smith.

Aug. 24th, 1941, Sunday. About 2.00pm, heavy explosion in harbour. Merchant ship loaded with coke for Ipswich struck mine. They say 18 men lost their lives. Plenty of coke being washed on beach.

Oct. 25th, 1941, Saturday. Siren sounded at 9.15pm. At 9.00pm enemy plane dropped bomb on Spa Pavilion, another in sea. No one hurt.

Jan. 17th, 1942, Saturday. About 3.15pm siren went. About 30 enemy planes over. Machine guns shot down balloon - I think it must have been the one over the Dooley tower.

Feb. 17th, 1942, Tuesday. About 1.30pm enemy planes dropped 2 bombs off Landguard Point as Mine Sweepers were coming in. Don't think there was any damage done.

April 16th, 1942, Easter Monday. About 9.30pm, hooter went. Searchlights up, gunfire from Landguard. No bombs dropped. All over by 10.30pm.

1942. I have been informed that Marriage's mill started making flour for the first time on Friday, Sept. 4th after being out of order since being burnt out.

June 2nd, 1943, Wednesday morning. About 5.30am, enemy planes over. Bombs dropped at Bawdsey Ferry on Potters houses, also at Trimley and Ipswich.

Aug. 23rd, 1943, Monday. About 10.30pm. Searchlights got plane in light. Lots of gunfire but plane went out to sea, very high up. During the night some people saw one come down in flames, fell at Chelmondiston just over the river. Jerry bailed out at Levington, taken to Felixstowe Police Station - so I am told.

Dec. 10th, 1943, Friday night. Siren went about 7.00 pm, heavy gun fire. Gas holder caught fire about 8.30pm. No other damage

Jan. 22nd, 1944, Saturday morning. About 5.00am. Very heavy gunfire all round. No bombs dropped near. Ten planes brought down, according to wireless reports. London was bombed.

Feb. 14th, 1944, Sunday. About 8.30pm very heavy gunfire all round. Flares and incendiaries dropping over Harwich way and at Landguard. Big fire at Harwich and Landguard Point.

June 1st, 1944, Thursday. Slept in at Air Station for 5 nights. Bed in Compressor House. Grub with troops. All O.K.

Aug. 25th, 1944, Friday night. About 9.00pm. Big bomber crashed into the sea in front of Cavendish Hotel (all lost). Heard it was one of our Halifaxes shot up over France. Saw same.

Aug. 31st, 1944, Thursday morning about 4.15am. Siren went. Doodlebugs over. Saw one come in from sea over Cork (lightship) way. Explosions heard long way off. No damage nearby.

Sept. 1st, 1944, Friday morning. At about 2.00am siren went. Flybombs over. One dropped Ipswich near Crane and Burnets. Lot of damage to homes nearby.

Flybombs came regularly between September 1944 and March 1945.

Nov. 7th, 1944, Tuesday. At 2.45 pm. Large bomber circled the dock. Right hand side wing seemed to come off and flew in flames. Plane came down near Martello tower (P) burning. Very large flames and smoke. Saw it all. Fell on Coastguard Cottages and burnt them out. 3 airmen killed in cottages also crew of plane.

May 8th, 1945, Tuesday. War finished with Germany. Had Tuesday and Wednesday off. Big celebrations throughout the

Country - all except Felixstowe, which was dry - not a pub open anywhere!

May 13th, 1945, Sunday. Two "E" boats arrived at Felixstowe. German officer was taken to Harwich by barge manned by W.R.N.S.

Aug. 14th/15th, Midnight. News came through that the war was over with Japs. Hooters went in harbour and searchlights up out Harwich way. Wednesday and Thursday, holiday. Very dull in Felixstowe.

END

Additional information to Diary enteries.

A. A Hampden of 144 Squadron hit a balloon cable over Harwich. Part of the port wing fell into the dock basin, but the main part fell onto the flour mill, killing the crew of four. Earlier in the month, on the night of the 3rd/4th, another Hampden from 44 Squadron ran into the Harwich barrage and crashed into the River Orwell.

B. A He111H-4 of Stab II/KG4 was shot down by a Blenheim of 23 Squadron. The port engine caught fire and the aircraft came down just off shore.

C. Do 17Z shot down by 17 Squadron Hurricanes. Came down at Rookery Farm, Cretingham.

Ḥꟿꟿꟿꟿꟿ BEEḤꟿVE.

During World War II a special branch of the Royal Navy was formed and designated Light Coastal Forces. It consisted of very fast Motor Torpedo Boats, Gun Boats and Motor Launches, the latter being much smaller craft, although all were made of wood.

They were based around the South East coast at places such as Gosport (HMS HORNET), Weymouth (HMS BEE), Lowestoft and Yarmouth - and Felixstowe (HMS BEEHIVE). Each base was named for an insect with a sting in its tail.

HMS BEEHIVE boasted twenty MTBs, sixteen MGBs, and four marine launches, which occupied the Felixstowe dock basin and Nos. 2 and 3 Hangars. Their job was to protect convoys in the North Sea and the English Channel and to harass and attack enemy ships off the Dutch, Belgian and French coasts.

Two hundred and fifty Naval Officers, including "aces" such as Lieutenant Commander Peter Scott, the Ornithologist, Lieutenant Commander Hutchins and Commander Ian Trelawny took over the Pier Hotel for use as an administrative centre, which eventually overflowed from the Officers' Mess into the Cliff Hotel in town.

The Pier Hotel, built by Colonel George Tomline in 1875, was later renamed THE LITTLE SHIPS, in honour of the small craft and valiant men who crewed and serviced them.

Note:
(The huge concrete red, grey, green and gold painted Tomline/ Pretyman Crest positioned above the main entrance to the Little Ships Hotel was salvaged following demolition in 1991

and donated to the Felixstowe Museum by The Felixstowe Dock and Railway Company.)

Commander I.C. Trelawny, D.S.C. and Bar, was Senior Officer of the 1st, 4th and then the 11th M.T.B. flotillas, and earned a reputation for regularly engaging in the longest sea fights in the Narrow Seas.

During 1944, the security of the waterfront was tightened and Felixstowe became one of the embarkation hards for the D-Day landings.

Stocks of medical equipment were stored in the cellars of the Little Ships, which served as an emergency sick bay. When an unexpected air raid occurred, S.B.S. (Sick Berth Staff) from M.S.Q. (Main Sick Quarters) at the Landguard end of base were detailed for duty in the cellars.

Should the main sick quarters be damaged, or destroyed, the reserve bay could be put to use, with medical personnel being available at both ends of HMS BEEHIVE, if required.

There was a separate naval unit attached to HMS BEEHIVE, called Boom Defence (trawler manned by the Navy), it being responsible for the boom or "net" stretching across river from Landguard to Harwich. A centre section could be opened to enable shipping to enter or leave the harbour.

On one occasion when craft were practising evolutions off Felixstowe, a vessel, striking some wreckage in the stern, started to take in water badly, the boat being of wood construction. Permission was given for the Captain to take the boat back to base at full speed, in order to keep the water down. This necessitated the boom defence across the river being opened by the skipper of a trawler guardship, which

Boom Defence WRENs
Suffolk Convalescent Home, Felixstowe, 1943.

Courtesy Toni Porter

took some minutes to complete. It was afterwards politely reported that the skipper became "quite giddy" as the MTB raced around in circles while at the same time signalling repeatedly for permission to enter port. The boat was eventually salvaged, repaired and placed back into service.

One afternoon, the attention of S.B.S. was drawn to a fighter pilot, with open parachute, at a very great height, being circled by a fighter plane. A strong offshore wind was blowing at the time. Air Sea Rescue was alerted to the fact that the pilot would eventually land in the sea, and they replied that a launch was on the way from Felixstowe dock basin to try to locate him.

Although the launch travelled at full speed, the strength of the wind carried the pilot over to the French coast, and it was assumed that he would face captivity until the end of the war.

On another occasion, a Flying Fortress bomber was shot down off the east coast by English gunners. The American crew suffered no serious injuries, although they were taken to the military hospital at Martlesham Heath. Having been paid just prior to boarding the aeroplane for a practice run and now being safely hospitalised, they proceeded to carefully empty pockets of rolls of soggy paper money, laying out each note to dry on three empty beds nearby.

American film actor Edward G. Robinson, who was in England at that time, had on the previous day dedicated the Flying Fortress, which, it was later reported, had not at the time flown an operational sortie.

A similar story involved Dakotas towing gliders which passed over Felixstowe on the way to Arnhem. Two complete glider crews, numbering ninety personnel, were rescued from the sea. Again, there were no serious injuries, although much concern was expressed by a Sergeant Major from one craft, who was carrying the unit pay, ready for handing out when the men had landed in Holland.

A four-engined bomber, returning in daylight from a raid upon enemy territory, crash-landed in Langer Road, Felixstowe, bounced into the air and ran into Coastguard Cottages and houses to the rear of Martello tower "P", close to the water's edge. Ammunition exploded in all directions and there was a huge fire which took several hours to extinguish. Members of the crew were killed while attempting to leap from the aeroplane prior to the crash, some landing against a double decker bus transporting Wrens to HMS BEEHIVE.

Aircraft wreckage, Coastguard Cottages, Langer Road.

One seriously burned crew member was treated in a nearby house before being rushed to Ipswich Hospital. The remainder, together with a number of R.A.F. personnel, were killed. Two ambulances from BEEHIVE, each carrying medical orderlies, were first on the scene and were later joined by a Civil Defence ambulance, fire engines, and members of the Salvation Army.

GERMAN SURRENDER

The Admiralty decided upon HMS BEEHIVE as the best place for the surrender of German E-boats. Two boats were to make a "token" surrender, and they were met by MTBs and officers, who boarded the German boats to escort them into the river and the Felixstowe Dock basin.

The photograph shows members of the Women's Royal Naval Service watching a German officer as he boarded the launch that was to take him to Harwich.

Wrens were also responsible for filling barrage balloons with dangerous mixture of hydrogen gas and air and often suffered severe burns which necessitated hospitalisation at Felixstowe Ferry. During the war, many were housed in the requisitioned seafront Suffolk Convalescent Home, which has since been demolished.

DISTRICT GUNNERS

Matt Rutterford, (?) Collins, (?) Studd, Ginger Rich and Ernie Bryant were local ex-artillery men and district gunners whose job it was to keep fort guns in working order, at the beginning of the second world war. When it became necessary, each of the above would take troopers, or squaddies, to any point along the East Coast to check, repair, or even remove and replace, the large weapons. For some time after the war, local children played on guns which remained in position.

Matt Rutterford's two boys had found and managed to operate the lever with which to traverse them. They also noted where 6-inch shells were stored behind locked iron doors, but, fortunately, were unable to gain access to same!

Position Firing instruments were kept in a building in front of the fort proper. These too were cared for by Rutterford.

In a Nissen hut, situated in the ditch just beneath the Victorian casemated battery for seven guns, was a collection of tools required for maintaining the huge weapons. Paddy Riley, who hailed from Ireland, was responsible for keeping these and other pieces of portable equipment in good repair. Every item was polished, 'so you could see your face in them, and each had a special hook or place. The abovementioned were military men of the old school and everything had to be just so.'

ROUGH RIDERS.

The Rutterford brothers recalled a Felixstowe-based regiment known as the "Rough Riders", who were positioned every two or three hundred yards along the top of Wolsey Gardens and on roof-tops of the Regal and Alexandra Hotels. They manned Bofor guns for defence against flying bombs.

'They used to rattle off rounds, because there were only five shells to a clip, which had to be pushed in as fast as possible. There was no need to actually have a direct hit. If the shells burst underneath the wing and upset the gyros, the bombs would just tail off into the sea.'

GAS BUSES

Derek Rutterford talked of buses powered by gas (1943). The containers, or bags, were on the roof of the bus - the gas ('smelling of rotten cabbages') being produced in a sort of corrugated tub, towed behind on a trailer. There was never enough power to drive up a hill, so passengers usually alighted, walked up the hill, boarding the bus again when it eventually arrived at the top.

DARELL DAY.

Until 1938, and again for approximately five years after the war, Darell Day was celebrated annually by the military, to commemorate the defeat of the 17th century Dutch attack on the "old" Landguard Fort. (Captain Nathaniel Darell was in charge of the victorious garrison.) This historical event was re-introduced in the early nineteen eighties by the Felixstowe History and Museum Society, following commencement of their campaign to preserve the then abandoned, derelict fortress. Darell Day, which usually began at mid-morning, was organised, by the military, for families of servicemen stationed at Landguard.

Until the late 1960s/early 1970s, the grounds stretched from the existing Viewing Area to Landguard Lodge, in Manor Terrace, and included land since taken up by a large Holiday Caravan Park. The event was sports-orientated, with all the usual games and races, tug-of-war and a 'tremendous bun fight'. High tea, set for about six o'clock in the evening, was followed late at night by a huge bonfire and fireworks.

At the end of the day, sweets, oranges, apples and other fruits were shared between exhausted, happy children. A great deal of effort went into organising this most popular victory celebration.

Note: Darell Day is organised annually by the F.H.& M.S. - albeit on a much smaller scale! Lack of space, funds and manpower prevents this small local society from repeating day long events introduced so many years ago.

THE RAVELIN BLOCK.

Ravelin is the name given to a triangular outwork in a fortification situated outside of the main surrounding ditch. Landguard's outwork was built by the Royal Engineers in 1878, following extensive renovations to the fort proper in 1875. The building has been occupied by the F.H.& M.S. since 1979 and now houses their popular museum collection.

The formerly open-ended corridor running through the centre of the Block once supported trolley lines, for the building was used not simply for stores and administration purposes, but also as a place in which to assemble and fill large circular mines with explosives before wheeling them on trolleys down to the jetty at the water's edge. The mines were primed just before being laid at intervals across the harbour mouth, and could be electrically operated from an area known as Mine Control, within the fort proper.

Entrance to Ravelin Block 1980.
Building now houses the Felixstowe Museum.

Photograph: Bunny Rayner

Mine Control is reached via a steep stairway leading to a narrow platform which offers a clear view of a two-mile stretch of water between Felixstowe and Harwich.

The aim was to protect the harbour and shores by preventing enemy shipping from sailing freely between the aforementioned towns and so on to London.

A rusting 19th century turntable used in an operation of this kind may still be seen at the rear of the Ravelin Block. Much of the narrow-gauge track is buried beneath Darell Road, which runs adjacent to the side of the building. It is still possible to see another section of the track which runs towards the jetty, if one looks inside a passage-way close to Darell Battery.

Since 1978, the writer, together with a small group of history enthusiasts, has worked tirelessly towards the restoration and opening to the public of the once abandoned, early 18th century, Grade I listed ancient monument (Landguard Fort).

A letter to Fortress House, in London, had, apparently, set its corridors "buzzing", for the fort, having been sealed for so many years, had been completely forgotten.

The group realised how fortunate they were to have been given an opportunity to form a good working relationship with, first, the Department of Environment and then, English Heritage.

Throughout the following years, representatives from the above-mentioned 'bodies' regularly travelled to Felixstowe to attend meetings, which were held in the derelict Ravelin Block, where icy blasts whistled through missing skylights, doors and windows, miserably failing to protect us from driving rain or blizzards.

It was in these dismal surroundings that some most important decisions were made.

Department officials liaised with Suffolk Coastal District Council regarding a change of use for the building. It was some weeks before the keys were finally handed to the History Society by Norman Hodgeson, who was Senior Architect with

Above:
Ravelin Block 1980
(now Landguard Room)

Left:
Vandalised partition, long
since repaired.
Now separates "Nautical"
from "HMS Beehive"
collection.

Photographs:
Bunny Rayner.

the Department of the Environment.

It was decided to repair skylights and re-asphalt the roof, to brick up the rear of the open-ended single storey Block, to replace double front doors, to reconnect electricity and water and to replace two smashed toilets, for members' use only. This work was carried out by the D. of E.

Our new headquarters - and the future Felixstowe Museum - needed a great deal of attention! For some years it had been left to vandals, who had seriously damaged the building. Almost every one of the nineteen rooms needed some renovation. To date, the F.H. & M.S. has carried out repairs to and decorated ten of them.

Months of weekend and evening work followed before it was possible to open one room to the public, in 1983. It was named THE LANDGUARD ROOM.

Throughout the following years, many more repairs and improvements were carried out to the Ravelin Block and the adjacent fortress. By 1985, the fort roof had been re-asphalted, at great cost; the inner and outer courtyards were cleared of rubble and undergrowth, and the front entrance was bricked up around a steel door, in an effort to deter illegal entrants and continuing vandalism. The surrounding ditch was also cleared and laid with shingle.

Bob Coleman was foreman in charge of re-asphalting the fort roof. One afternoon, having emerged from the fort interior after taking a group of visitors on a guided tour, the author was stopped by Bob, who expressed an interest in History Society activities. What he actually said was,

'I wouldn't mind joining your lot, when I retire in a few months time.'

He was immediately enrolled! Bob became a guide in 1986 and is still with us at the time of writing!

Members of the F.H. & M.S. were given permission to escort small, interested groups around the fort interior in 1985. There were certain rules to follow, such as: no more than fifteen per group, and no unaccompanied children.

For months society members worked on a purely voluntary basis, before realising that here was a way in which funds could be raised for the provision and maintenance of a museum collection. A charge of fifty pence was introduced!

It was not long before our too few guides were becoming overworked! Visitors formed queues to look inside the fort proper. Many were prepared to wait for an hour, if necessary. In 1985 there were three guides, namely: Bunny and Doreen Rayner and David Tolliday. Bob Coleman and Tony Rayner joined the team in 1986. In 1995 we numbered eight! Nine years ago, it took approximately half an hour to conduct a party around the fort interior. Today, it will take almost one hour and fifteen minutes to complete the same route .... due to a great deal of additional historical information having been unearthed.

ENGINE ROOM AND SEARCHLIGHTS.

An engine room was linked to the rear of the Ravelin Block by a railway track, still to be seen today. Electric power for the searchlights was provided by generators housed in the engine room; one generator per light. Each had an output voltage of about 90 volts D.C. and could supply 250 amps. Generators were driven at 1000 r.p.m. by a 4 cylinder Crossley petrol/paraffin engine, started up by using petrol as a fuel. When the engine had reached operating temperature, the fuel supply was changed over to paraffin. Before closing down, the fuel was changed back to petrol, so that all of the fuel line and the carburettor contained petrol, ready for the next start.

Getting started was quite a performance. Each cylinder had a relief tap, which had to be opened, to reduce the compression ratio, to allow easier turning over; for each cylinder, a small container and a stopcock allowed about a tablespoonful of petrol to be fed in before starting. Cranking was by hand; as soon as the engine fired, the relief taps had to be closed.

The three remaining concrete searchlight towers, to the right of Darell's Battery, housed fighting lights with narrow beams. Each light was traversed by remote control from the Command Post and was aimed at the bow-wave of a target vessel. At each light, an operator was stationed to strike "arc" when commanded, to ensure correct operation of the arc lamp, and to change the carbons (which were fully consumed after about thirty minutes of operation). Later models had automatic feed and even changing of the carbons.

In the late 1940s, "Butchy" Baker was in charge of the Engine Room. It is said he was a brilliant Engineer who could strip down any such machine and build it up again. "Butchy" would often go into the Master Gunner's office for a mug of tea and a cigarette. There was a small coke fire in there and he would casually put his hand into it, to take out a red hot coal to light his cigarette. He would then calmly put it back into the fire. There was never a mark on his fingers!

OPERATIONS ROOM DISCOVERED

An exciting discovery was made in August, 1995, when workmen began to test woodwork and floorboards in the Victorian Casemated battery for seven guns.

Approximately fifty years ago, one of the batteries had been converted into an Ops Room. At first, it was thought to date from the 1939/1945 war. Plans which later came to light, however, confirm conversion from barrack room to Ops Room as having taken place in 1951, at the time of the "cold war".

An oval-shaped table, covered with layers of dirt, dust and pigeon droppings, stands in the centre of the room, and may have supported a map of the entire coastline. It is tilted towards a platform (reached by way of eight wooden steps), from where directions/orders may well have been given.

A plan shows former telex message receiving and various other rooms. Tote and message boards, together with other vital pieces of equipment, have disappeared, of course, but could, I am reliably informed, quite easily be recovered, in order to recreate the whole for visitor attraction purposes.

This room was obviously sealed up prior to the army vacating the fort in 1956/7.

SEAWARD DEFENCE HEADQUARTERS.

(Information courtesy of J.Roper)

During WWII the seaward defences of the area were controlled by the Fire Commander from his observation post on top of Landguard Fort, and from a plotting room in the old magazines. This was in conjunction with the other services, using both Radar and visual lookouts.

In the late 1940s and early 1950s various new ideas came into being, for the control of Coast Defences, one of these being S.D.H.Q. (Seaward Defence Head Quarters).

This was a control room with a central plotting area which enabled representatives of various services to see what was happening in the area and to prepare the appropriate counter measures to defend the coastline.

The information passed to the S.D.H.Q. from Radar and lookouts was mainly by telephone, although radio was used as well.

J.Roper of Felixstowe took part in exercises which were held to test this system, he being No.2 of a C.A. Mk1 Radar (early warning set) at Beacon Hill, Dovercourt, reporting to S.D.H.Q. by telephone, with a radio set as back-up if the telephone lines went down.

He also worked on other exercises, plotting on the table at S.D.H.Q. within the fort, at one time with the Wrens plus two gunners carrying out plotting duties.

Different types and shape of plotting table were tried out. These were gridded in the Geo. reference against the National Grid that had previously been used for plotting.

The C.A. Mk2 was an early warning radar set in a portable cabin, with a single parabolic dish aerial. There was one on the roof of Landguard Fort, one at Beacon Hill, Dovercourt, and one at Brackenbury Fort. These sets were in contact with S.D.H.Q. by telephone.

There was a C.A. Mk22, fire control Radar set which had twin parabolic dish aerials at the top of a 60 feet steel tower. There was also an enclosed position with a visual director for bearing only, at the top of the tower. The controls, Radar screens for range and bearing, together with various ancillary equipment were all situated in a concrete blockhouse next to the base of the tower.

This set was positioned close to the M.T. garage, to the left of the original road over the seawall, leading to Landguard Fort. A patch of rough grass and brambles denotes the position now.

One of the lining up points for the C.A. Mk11 Radar was Fort Rough (sea fort) with a bearing of 113^0 06'.

Amongst the equipment in the blockhouse was a Coast Artillery Table that could mechanically take up the displacement of the Radar from the guns, thus enabling engagement of a target with a correct range and bearing from the guns. This information was transmitted electrically by a means known as "magslip".

Photograph taken in front of 6-inch Mk24 gun at Fan Bay Battery, Wanston, Dover. June 1950.
"P" and "S" BATTERIES, 419 COAST REGIMENT
Unless otherwise stated all are Felixstowe men.

Rear Rank. Left to right.
L/Bdr. Gardner, Bdr. Studd, Bdr. Driver, Bdr. Finbow, Gnr....
Gnr. ...

Centre Rank.
Gnr. Proctor, Gnr. Barber, L/Bdr.... L/Bdr. Boon, Sgt. Swan (Ipswich), B.Q.M.S. Hearn, B.Q.M.S. Smith (Trimley. Electrician), WOII. Randle, Sgt.... (Kirton), Sgt. Lewis, L/Bdr. Andrews, Gnr....

Front Rank.
WOII. Godfrey, WOII. Warner, Capt...., Capt. Cocksedge (Ipswich), Major Balham, Capt. Piper (Little Bealings), Lt...., WOII. Sneddon (Reg . Soldier), WOII. Williams.

419 COAST REGIMENT. ROYAL ARTILLERY. TERRITORIAL ARMY.

This regiment was formed in 1947 when the Territorial Army was re-activated after World War II.

"P" and "S" Batteries.

Attended their drill nights at the Drill Hall, Garrison Lane, Felixstowe, which was also Battalion Head Quarters. They were responsible for manning the two 6-inch Mk24 guns of the Right Battery, and for manning the two twin 6-pounder quick firing guns of Darell Battery, together with the radars, searchlights etc., at Landguard Fort.

"R" and "H.Q." Batteries.

Attended their drill nights at the Drill Hall, Beacon Hill, Dovercourt, which was alson Regimental Head Quarters. They were responsible for manning the 6-inch Mk24 and the twin 6-pounder quick firing guns at Beacon Hill.

In 1956 after Coast Artillery was "stood down" the 419 Coast Regiment was amalgamated with the 358 Suffolk Yeomanry Field Regiment R.A. (T.A.)., with H.Q. at Bury St. Edmunds. Following various retirements, redundancies and reductions in rank they became the two troops of "R" Battery, firing 25-pounder Field Guns; a great difference to being Concrete Gunners, as Coast Artillery was known.

In 1961 the 358th (Suffolk Yeomanry) was amalgamated with the 284th (K.O.R.R. Norfolk Yeomanry) thus becoming the 308th (Suffolk and Norfolk Yeomanry) Field Regiment, R.A. (T.A.). "R" Battery was then amalgamated with "P" Battery at Ipswich, forming one troop of that Battery. Since then there have been various alterations and amalgamations but there are still Artillery units at Ipswich and Bury St. Edmunds.

LANDGUARD FORT TRUST

The Landguard Fort Trust was formed through the Landguard Forum (1986), the latter being a body set up by Suffolk Coastal District Council, which came to recognise the monument's potential as a tourist attraction.

In brief, the idea behind a Landguard Forum was to draw together interested parties, such as the Suffolk Wildlife Trust, Suffolk County Council, English Heritage, The Felixstowe History and Museum Society, and the Port of Felixstowe, with a view to exchanging ideas and ironing out possible problems, prior to initiating a feasibility study.

Four options emerged from the feasibility study; the least expensive being to form a Trust to raise funds and to manage the monument.

A Trust was officially formed in 1995.

Landguard Fort will be closed to the public throughout 1996, while extensive repairs are carried out to the interior, in order to make it safe for visitors to wander at will in 1997. (The Felixstowe Museum will remain open as usual.) Barrack rooms, former Officers' quarters, inner and outer courtyards, magazine and other areas will be cleared, railings will be replaced and walkways and staircases made more easily accessible.

The Fire Command Post situated on top of the fort roof will also be renovated. There are plans to convert a ground floor barrack room, inner courtyard, into a tea room, while others could become craft shops.

Original casemates in the outer courtyard may well be

used for exhibition purposes. Hopefully, trustees will recognise the value in retaining an existing eighteenth century character.

Landguard Fort, largest coastal fortification in East Anglia, is set to become one of the most popular visitor attractions in the country .... due largely to that one small step, taken by a group of eight local history enthusiasts seventeen years ago. Keeping alive an interest in the monument has been a challenging, rewarding task, and it is with a mixture of sadness and hope that management has been handed over to the Landguard Fort Trust.

Doreen Rayner,
Secretary, The Felixstowe History and Museum Society,
Hon. Curator, Felixstowe Museum.
Tour Guide 1985 - 1995.

ANCIENT FORTIFICATIONS.

BLOCKHOUSES were first noted at Landguard between 1540 and 1547.

One at the "Poynte", facing seawards. Another at Garrison Rood Springs, thought to be in the vicinity of the old (now demolished) Dooley Fort/Walton Battery.

1553.   "Ordinaunce and Municon" removed to Tower of London.
1588.   End of Armada scare.
        The following are extracts from the Ipswich Chamberlain's yearly accounts.

Item   To Master Gregory for drawings of a platforme for the bulworke at Langer.

Item   For fetching the same platforme from him and carrying it to Sur Phelipp Parker.

Item   26th October. To Mistress Lymfilde for wyne, sugar, cakes and beere bestowed upon Sur P. Parker and his men.

Item   19 Dec. To Mistress Lymfilde for a supper and a breakfaste and hors meate bestowed upon Sur P. Parker and his men.

Item   For the hier of 7 horse to Langer when the Knights and the rest of the gentlemen rid thether, for to carye their muskettes and there to shoot at their apoyntments.

THE OLD FORT.

1626.　　OLD FORT built of turf and wood. Four bastions and surrounding ditch.
Governor: The Earl of Holland.
Troops quartered in the fort came under their own Commander, except for fort defence.
Arrangements were always in hand for rapid reinforcement.

In the time of King James II, the old fort was held by one hundred men of Colonel Hale's regiment, backed up by brigades at Ipswich and Colchester, each of two Regiments of Horse and one Regiment of Dragoons (mounted infantry).

1667.　　Bastions enlarged. Ditch rivetted in brick.
Fort attacked by the Dutch, July 2nd, 1667.
Repelled by Nathaniel Darell and garrison.
At the time of the Dutch attack, the two Coys. of the Duke of York's were backed by 4 Coys at Harwich and the Militia (Horse and Foot) assembled at Walton.

The Master Gunner was supported by an additional staff of three to help work the 18 Culverins, 23 Demi-Cannon, 9 Sakers, 4 Minion and 5 brand new three-pounders.

1703.　　Master Gunner - James Hubbard.
Master General of the Ordnance - The Duke of Marlborough.

90

THE NEW FORT.

1716. Ancient pieces were removed to make way for 15 x new twenty- four-pounders and 5 x six- pounders.

1717. Work commenced on "NEW FORT"
A sea battery (without corner bastions) equipped with South Tower, counterscarpe galleries, twenty guns, modest barrack block, increased in size circa 1730s.

1744. Now a four bastion defence surrounded by a ditch. Within its walls a barrack block, hospital, Lieutenant Governor's residence, Officers' quarters, and chapel above main gate.
Beauclerk's Battery built.

1745. Guns worked by an Invalid Company.

1763. Invalids still being trained by Master Gunner and Company.

1771. Introduction of the "professionals". Master Gunner and staff replaced by Royal Artillery personnel detached from Woolwich - one from Captain Hind's Company and two from Captain Buchanan's.

1778. Retrenched camp laid out. Two Redoubts facing channel. Beauclerk's Battery extended left and right to take additional 14 cannon.
Total of 115 cannon.
Engineer in charge was Thomas Hyde Page.

1794. Suffolk and Essex incorporated into a new No.3

District. Area re-armed.
Master Gunner given an NCO and 10 gunners.
Increased responsibilities.
In the fort: 11 x 42-pounders (heavy metal)
                11 x 32-pounders
                20 x 18-pounders - Carronades for
                close quarter work.

At Harwich a Battery of 8 x 24-pounders.
At Holesly Bay and Deben area there were no less than 60 x 24-pounders.

With peace the then Master Gunner, James Barron, reduced to having two invalid gunners.

1795.   Improvements carried out to fort walls.
South facing ramparts strengthened and fitted with traversing platforms.
Beauclerk's fitted with traversing platforms.

ARMAMENT

14	32-Pounders
2	12-Pounders
1	6-Pounder
20	12-Pounder Carronades
11	42-Pounders on Beauclerks Battery.
2	18-Pounders.

1807   Ramparts strengthened to take recoil of 32-Pounders.

1875   Interior buildings and chapel demolished. Replaced with semicircular Keep to form inner and outer with casemated battery for seven guns (rifled

muzzle loaders
Fronted at ditch level by a Caponier and solid brick hemispherical structure, designed to deflect pointed shells/cannon balls, to help protect magazine area.

1875.   Manually controlled minefield approved.
Ravelin Block, Pier, ancillary test rooms, magazines and cable ponds built.

1880.   Landguard Fort becomes (Royal) Artillery, rather than Infantry responsibility.

1891.   Left Battery completed

1901.   First Engine House built, to generate electricity for searchlights and fort interior.

1901.   Construction of Minefield Battery, later renamed Darell's Battery. Existing concrete towers either side built 1930s.

1901.   Right Battery completed.

circa 1910. Rifled Muzzle Loaders removed from fort interior.

1914   Maps in existence showing Landguard Fort and Felixstowe defensive positions.

1930s   Commencement of 2 & 3 storey Barrack Blocks.

1940's   Maps showing defensive positions, gun emplacements, new engine room.Minefield Control Station, Barracks and Rifle Ranges.

1951   Map showing Fortress Plotting Room. S.D.H.O.

1956.   Army vacated. Fortress sealed.

1985   Commencement of guided tours of fort interior courtesy of F.H. & M.S. Permission of English Heritage.

1995   Formation of Landguard Fort Trust. Monument destined to become a Visitor Attraction.